Lars Brownworth is an author, speaker, broadcaster, and teacher based in Maryland, USA. He has written for the *Wall Street Journal* and been profiled in the *New York Times,* which likened him to some of history's great popularizers. His books include I*n Distant Lands, Lost to the West, The Normans* and *The Sea Wolves.*

THE CAESARS

Volume I

JULIUS CAESAR
ROMAN COLOSSUS

LARS BROWNWORTH

CRUX
PUBLISHING

First published in the United Kingdom in 2021
by Crux Publishing Ltd.
ISBN: 978-1-909979-87-1

Requests for permission to reproduce material from this
work should be sent to
hello@cruxpublishing.co.uk

For Ellertsen

CONTENTS

CAST OF CHARACTERS

Ariovistus – *Germanic warlord who controlled the territory of what is now Flanders*

Aurelia Caesar – *Mother of Julius Caesar*

Bibulus – *Son-in-law of Cato and bitter enemy of Caesar; co-consul with Caesar in 59 BC*

Brutus – *Descendant of the founder of the Republic, Caesar's most famous assassin*

Caesarion – *Son of Julius Caesar and Cleopatra*

Calpurnia – *Fourth wife of Julius Caesar*

Cassius Longinus – *Brother-in-law of Brutus, supporter of Pompey and one of Caesar's three main assassins*

Cassivellaunus – *British tribal chief who commanded the forces opposing Caesar's invasion of Britain*

Catiline – *Roman patrician who attempted to overthrow the Republic but was stopped by Cicero*

Cato the Younger – *Conservative Roman senator known for his Stoic philosophy and his opposition to Caesar*

Cicero – *Roman statesman and orator, occasional ally of Caesar*

Cinna – *Colleague of Gaius Marius and father of Caesar's wife Cornelia*

Cleopatra – *Pharaoh of Egypt and Caesar's lover*

Clodius – *Wild patrician and rabble-rouser, attempted to seduce one of Caesar's wives*

Cornelia – *Second wife of Julius Caesar and mother of Julia*

Cossutia – *First wife of Julius Caesar. The two were engaged, but there is dispute over whether or not the marriage ever took place.*

Crassus – *The wealthiest man in Rome and one of the three Triumvirs*

Decimus Brutus – *Cousin of Marcus Junius Brutus, close friend of Caesar, and one of Caesar's three main assassins*

Gaius Marius – *Roman general and maternal uncle of Julius Caesar, became consul seven times, seized Rome by force in a bloody coup*
Julia – *Aunt of Julius Caesar, wife of Gaius Marius*
Julia – *Daughter of Julius Caesar and Cornelia; Caesar's only legitimate child. Married Pompey the Great*
Lucius Junius Brutus – *Founder of the Republic, distant ancestor of Caesar's most famous assassin*
Marcus Lepidus – *Roman senator and ally of Julius Caesar*
Mark Antony – *One of Caesar's most trusted lieutenants*
Mithridates – *King of Pontus, known as the Poison King; invaded Roman territory three times*
Octavius – *Grand-nephew of Caesar, future emperor Augustus*
Pharnaces – *Son of Mithridates. His quick defeat at the hands of Caesar prompted the famous line "veni, vidi, vici"*
Pompeia – *Third wife of Julius Caesar, granddaughter of Sulla*
Pompey the Great – *Roman general and Caesar's main rival*
Ptolemy 13th – *Husband and younger brother of Cleopatra, responsible for the murder of Pompey the Great*
Ptolemy 14th – *Husband and youngest brother of Cleopatra*
Servillia – *Favourite mistress of Caesar and mother of Marcus Junius Brutus*
Spartacus – *Escaped gladiator who led a major slave revolt. Killed by Crassus*
Sulla – *Roman general who marched on Rome and made himself dictator for life. Rival of Gaius Marius*
Titus Milo – *Gang leader hired by Pompey to neutralise Clodius*
Varro – *Roman scholar and partisan of Pompey, first to define the concept of "liberal arts"*
Vercingetorix – *Gallic chieftain who united the Gauls against Caesar*

Chapter 1

THE SUBURRA

"The affairs of Rome are founded upon her ancient customs and the quality of her men"

-Ennius

"If a child dies young, one should console himself easily… If he dies in the cradle, one doesn't even pay attention". Such was the advice of the Roman statesman Cicero, reflecting the harsh reality of infant mortality during the last century of the Roman Republic.[1] One third of children born did not survive their first year, half didn't make it to puberty. The celebration was muted, therefore, on a warm day in early July, 100 B.C. when Aurelia Caesar gave birth to a son. The crying infant, newly washed and swaddled, was scooped up by his father and held in the air, signifying his official acceptance into the Julii family. Nine days later he was given the same name as his father – Gaius Julius Caesar – and a good luck charm called a bulla was draped across his neck[2].

The family into which Julius Caesar was born predated Rome itself. They claimed descent from Julius, grandson of the goddess Venus and son of Aeneas, the mythical founder of the Roman people[3]. In their blood the divine and human origins of Rome met,

---

[1] Cicero wrote this a month after his beloved daughter Tullia had died in childbirth. His point was to amplify his own pain despite the common occurrence of losing a child. There was no specific word for "baby" in Latin.

[2] The origin of the name 'Caesar' (*hairy*) was disputed even in ancient times. It was attributed variously to a particularly shaggy ancestor, one who was cut out of a dead mother, or – since it's similar to the Moorish word – an elephant that his grandfather had killed in Africa. Julius Caesar's later use of an elephant on a coin was a nod to this story.

[3] Julius Caesar could consider himself a distant cousin of Romulus.

and fittingly, there were Julians intertwined with the earliest legends of the city. A member of the family had allegedly served Romulus, and another had been one of the first consuls after the foundation of the Republic. There wasn't a single important government job that the family hadn't filled; at least twelve had served as consuls, and one had even been a dictator[4].

Such a glittering pedigree was to be celebrated, and the Julian home served as an appropriate monument to the greatness of the Julian name. A columned portico lined the entrance like some grand temple, drawing visitors toward the sacred space within. Beyond lay the atrium, a vast hall lined with the wax death masks of past Julians, stretching back in time to the first Julian and the divine matriarch, Venus.

The problem with the Julian past, however, was that it was very much in the past. There was a conspicuous lack of modern entrants into the grand panoply of figures, and the outside of the house itself was an uncomfortable witness to just how far the family had fallen. What had once been a fashionable neighbourhood was now an overcrowded slum[5]. Ramshackle tenement buildings with peeling paint and rotting wood squatted next to brothels, taverns and a few dilapidated temples. There was more than a whiff of decay to it all. In the past two centuries, barely two members of gens Julii had managed to rise to high office, and the family's finances had declined precipitously. Not even the most glittering patrician credentials could shield against the whims of fortune.

As head of the family – paterfamilias – it was up to the elder Caesar to reverse this trend. He managed to contract a marriage with Aurelia, the daughter of an equally blue-blooded family, and took up service in the army – the natural launching pad of a political career. Unfortunately, in the bloodsport of Roman politics, money, ambition, and talent were necessary ingredients, and the elder Caesar lacked all three.

---

[4] Dictator was an elected position in the Roman Republic. In times of crisis dictators were appointed for a period of six months or less.
[5] Caesar's house was located roughly where the Colosseum now stands.

What he did have was an unmarried sister named Julia, and, as it turned out, she was the key to a dramatic reversal of family fortunes. Ten years before Caesar was born, she married the rising star of the Roman world, the fabulously wealthy and volcanically destructive Gaius Marius.

Rome had never seen anyone quite like Marius. Born in 157 BC into a modestly wealthy family from Arpinum, a dusty central Italian town, he had a knack for both seizing opportunities and unceasing self-promotion. This was already apparent by the time he was a teenager when he managed to catch a falling eagle's nest in his cloak. Discovering that there was a clutch of seven chicks inside – an unheard of rarity – he immediately announced that it was a sign from Jupiter (whose symbol the bird was) that he would reach the consulship seven times[6]. It was a thought that would have horrified any self-respecting Republican. Although Rome was a city where ambition was encouraged, there was something disturbing about too much of it. Excessive drive had an echo of despotism that was unseemly in an adult and downright ridiculous in an adolescent. It was true that great men in the past had served as consul more than once, and a few had even been elected three times. But seven was beyond the pale. Marius might as well have declared his intent to be king[7].

His path to greatness had unsurprisingly been through the army, the usual starting point for a political career. He rose quickly through the ranks, ultimately being appointed governor of Hispania Ulterior – what is today southern Spain. Anyone could see that he was a man on the make, and when he returned from Spain and married Julius Caesar's aunt, Julia, it was welcomed by both families: Marius gained entry into the rarified social circles usually reserved for patricians, and the cash-strapped Julian clan found political relevance.

---

[6] At least that's the story Marius told. He made the eagle the official symbol of the Roman army.

[7] The title of 'King' was the ultimate taboo in Roman politics. Having rid themselves of the monarchy in the early sixth century, the Romans were determined not to fall back into it. To take just one example, Lucius Junius Brutus, the founder of the Republic, executed his own sons when they attempted to restore the monarchy.

The blue blood now surrounding him, however, failed to appreciably change his brash character. He was the quintessential 'new man', an outsider who played up his rustic virtues and homespun values to curry favour with the masses[8]. He promised to break through the crusty aristocratic hold on power without any compromise. His political philosophy was summed up in a piece of advice he gave to one eastern king, "either be stronger than Rome or obey its commands". In politics and everything else Marius intended to be the strongest.

He was as good as his word. Within a few years he had become the most powerful man in Rome, universally recognized as the preeminent figure of the Republic. The Julians had clearly hitched their wagon to the right star. Political offices and favours began to be sprinkled throughout the family. Julius Caesar's father was made governor of Asia, and his uncle served as Consul.

Meanwhile, Marius' career played out like a Hollywood script. Using a convenient military crisis, he managed to become elected consul, a difficult achievement for a Roman with no prestigious ancestors. This was the virtual peak of power in the Republic, the singular achievement of a political life. Traditionally, after a year of service – the more sedate the better – an ex-consul was expected to fade gracefully into a comfortable retirement or embrace the role of elder statesman in the ranks of the Senate. Marius, however, wanted considerably more. Before his tenure expired he had managed to push through a series of reforms which abolished the property requirement to serve in the army. This instantly solved the manpower issues of the army, and opened up a huge recruiting pool among the city's poor. More importantly, it effectively transferred the loyalty of the soldiers from Rome to himself[9].

The move undid more than four centuries of Roman tradition, but it was just the start of Marius' ambitions. When several Germanic tribes crossed the Alps and invaded Italy, swatting aside several Roman armies along the way, Marius had ridden to the rescue.

[8] The term *novus homo* literally meant a man who was holding an important magistracy for the first time in his family's history.
[9] Land was the usual reward for military service, handed out to veterans by their generals.

In one climactic battle he had left more than three hundred thousand barbarian corpses on the field and earned the nickname the 'Third Founder of Rome' by the rapturously grateful capital[10]. It should have been the crowning moment of his career, but Marius still remained unsatisfied. Over the next few years he stormed his way to six total consulships, trampling tradition, and any pretense of legality in the process. The unprecedented number of awards and offices left even his most ardent supporters nervous, and the Senate outraged.

The anti-Marians found an unlikely champion in Lucius Cornelius Sulla, one of Marius' erstwhile lieutenants. Sulla was of rarefied patrician stock, but his family had long before fallen into poverty. In his youth, he had lived in an apartment block with freed slaves, barely able to afford the rent. His escape from the slums was only made possible by the fortuitous deaths of his stepmother and mistress, both of whom left all they had to him[11].

The sudden wealth made a political career possible. Sulla began it by joining one of Marius' campaigns in North Africa, hoping to establish a reputation that would be remembered by voters during an election. With his piercing blue eyes and shock of blonde hair, Sulla cut an impressive figure, and his unerring tactical sense soon attracted the attention of the great general. He rose to become the second-in-command, and was so trusted by Marius that Marius left him in charge of the North African army when he returned to Rome to stand for an election.

Sulla was, in many ways, the opposite of his boss. Where Marius was brash, Sulla was charming, and where Marius trumpeted his peasant virtues, Sulla oozed aristocratic hauteur. What they had in common, however, was their all-consuming ambition, and Marius' insistence on taking the credit even for the victories that Sulla engineered inevitably made them enemies.

---

[10] The first founder, of course, was Romulus. The second was the dictator Marcus Furius Camilus who had saved the city from a massive Gaulish invasion in the fourth century BC.

[11] There were rumors both at the time and afterwards that these deaths were a little *too* fortunate for Sulla, but nothing was ever proved.

Although Sulla never lost his penchant for low tastes – including his embarrassing habit of dining with actors – the Senate found him infinitely preferable to the populist Marius. They lost no time in promoting his career at the expense of Marius, and as Sulla's star rose, the ageing general seemed to grow more unstable. When a serious revolt of Italian allies broke out against Rome, Marius expected to be named supreme commander, and was deeply insulted when the Senate awarded the title to his rival Sulla instead.

Marius, who had probably also suffered a stroke, retired in a huff to one of his estates to wait for the Senate to realize that Sulla was in over his head, and repent of its mistake. The moment another crisis presented itself, he was sure his name would be on everyone's lips.

He didn't have long to wait. Rome's desperate struggle against its former Italian allies attracted the attention of Mithridates, the ambitious eastern king of Pontus, a small kingdom on the southern coast of the Black Sea[12]. The flamboyant Mithridates, who had a habit of dressing in golden armor and faux Hercules attire complete with lion-skin, claimed descent from both the Persian king Cyrus the Great and at least two generals of Alexander the Great. He was popularly known as the 'Poison King', since at the tender age of thirteen, he had seen his father die from poisoning, and understandably became obsessed with avoiding the same fate. He quickly built up the ancient world's largest collection of poisons and supposedly experimented with them on prisoners who had been condemned to death. He was popularly believed to have acquired an immunity by the novel method of ingesting small amounts of every known poison over a period of time. It was even whispered that he had concocted a universal antidote, although why he would have needed one was never explained[13].

Mithridates had been attempting to enlarge his kingdom for years, but wasn't considered a credible threat. With his ridiculous costumes and penchant for dirty tricks – some of his more creative tactics included launching beehives at opposing infantry and

---

[12] Pontus is in present-day northeastern Turkey.
[13] The antidote contained garlic, cinnamon, charcoal, ginger, parsley, opium, and duck blood – among other secret ingredients.

catapulting rotting corpses over city walls to spread disease – he was more comical than threatening. But Mithridates had chosen his moment perfectly. The Romans were desperately unpopular in the East, and while Rome had been distracted fighting its own allies on the Italian peninsula, Mithridates had organized an uprising with the most terrible consequences: in a single day more than 80,000 Romans throughout the East- including women and children – were butchered. One panicked historian claimed that by nightfall no one with even a single drop of Roman blood had been left alive. Roman control of the east evaporated and Mithridates swept into Athens.

The scale of the disaster panicked the entire Republic. The Italian revolt – nicknamed The Social War – which had been winding down for some time, was hastily concluded[14]. Gaius Marius, confident that his hour had arrived, immediately returned to Rome. However, he failed to convince the people of his suitability for the supreme command: his insistence on taking off his shirt and training with the new recruits despite being nearly 70 and semi-obese, didn't do him any favors. Once again, the Senate awarded supreme command to his great enemy, Sulla.

This final rejection was too much for Marius to bear. Perhaps he actually believed the prophecy that he would be consul seven times, or perhaps, like most ageing stars, he missed the spotlight and was unable to bow out gracefully. Before Sulla had a chance to take up his command, Marius led an armed band into the forum and demanded that he be given the charge against Mithridates. Some of his thugs attacked Sulla's supporters and in the confusion several people – including a consul's son – were killed. Sulla himself only escaped by cleverly fleeing to Marius' nearby house, the one place into which the mob was reluctant to smash its way. Fortunately for Sulla, the old general wasn't interested in his rival's life, only his command, which was quickly granted.

In a deeply ironic twist, however, Marius now found out that he had seriously overplayed his hand. His own reforms had made

---

[14] Julius Caesar's uncle, Lucius Caesar, effectively ended it by offering full citizenship to Rome's former allies.

the Roman army what it now was: clients loyal to their commanders instead of the state – and they overwhelmingly saw Sulla as their commander. Marius' veterans had long since retired; it was Sulla who had been handing out rewards for the past decade. No decree from Rome could compete with that. When Marius sent representatives to the army where it was camped outside of Rome to announce his command, they were quickly murdered. Sulla, on the other hand, was greeted rapturously when he appeared a few days later.

Sulla now faced the most fateful moment of his career. Although he had legally obtained his command, he could hardly leave for the east with Marius in charge of Rome. On the other hand, Marius could clearly not be evicted from Rome without force. Any attempt to do so would surely start a civil war. Yet Sulla barely hesitated. Instead of marching towards Mithridates, he turned his six legions on the capital. For the first time in the four and a half centuries of the Republic's existence a Roman general marched on Rome[15].

Marius was taken completely by surprise. His hastily improvised defense – a disorganised rabble consisting of gladiators and felons – was easily beaten and he was forced into a humiliating flight. Fortunately for everyone, Sulla wasn't interested in staying in Rome for long. He was acutely aware of his growing unpopularity, and the outrage he had caused by marching on Rome. Leaving was the only sensible action. Even his supporters in the Senate were appalled by what he had done, and he was eager to get to grips with Mithridates. He only stayed long enough to pass two quick resolutions. His command was officially confirmed, and Gaius Marius was declared a public enemy. To most Romans, however, it was Sulla himself who was the outlaw.

Marius, meanwhile, had escaped to Africa where he was busy plotting his return. He made common cause with an exiled consul named Cinna, and as soon as Sulla was gone, they returned to Italy as saviors. The euphoria didn't last long. Marius was keen on only one thing: revenge. A cloud of terror descended on the city and anyone he considered an enemy faced a nasty end. The Senate, most of

---

[15] With one exception, Sulla's horrified officers deserted, but tellingly the soldiers showed no qualms about attacking Rome.

whose members had consistently supported Sulla, was systematically purged. He and Cinna were made consuls without the bother of an election and despite Marius being increasingly unhinged. The seventh consulship had fulfilled the prophecy, but it was a sad dénouement to the career of a man who had once been hailed as Rome's 'Third Founder'. The end came quickly. To everyone's relief Marius expired only seventeen days later.

His death brought an end to most of the killing, but it did nothing to relieve the general anxiety. With Cinna still in control of Rome, and Sulla somewhere at the head of six legions, everyone in Rome was forced to make a choice between the Marian and Sullan camps.

Chapter 2

FLAMEN DIALIS

"Experience is the teacher of all things"

- Caesar

L ike most of Rome, Julius Caesar's extended family was split, and the elder Caesar now had the difficult task of protecting his children's interests in the overheated political climate. He had already taken several steps to ensure their careers. Having returned from his governorship a wealthy man, he had put his money at the disposal of tutors to educate his remarkable son. A cloud of rhetoricians – including a Gaul named Marcus Antonius Gripho, widely considered Rome's finest orator – had descended on the Julian home. From the beginning, Julius Caesar was a quick student. An iron discipline instilled by his mother was reinforced by an often brutal educational regimen. Like other boys of his class, school could begin at sunrise and last till dusk with few breaks to ease the strain. Schooling was overseen by tutors who reinforced their lessons with whips; a slow or incorrect answer could result in a beating.

The final piece of Caesar's education was provided by his family home itself. All those wax masks on display instilled an acute awareness of his ancestry and, perhaps, a belief in his own destiny. One of his earliest compositions was an essay in praise of the demigod Hercules, a mortal man who had managed to storm his way into heaven.

The most important influence on young Caesar's life was his mother, Aurelia. From equally patrician roots as her husband, she was every inch the proper Roman matron. Each aspect of young Caesar's life was strictly regulated – his games as relentlessly as his studies. Under such auspices, his childhood cannot have been very pleasant, but it produced a disciplined man. In any case it was soon over.

While lacing up his sandals one morning in 85 B.C. – a year after Marius expired – Gaius Julius Caesar the Elder suddenly died[16]. A mild man of limited ambition and talent, the elder Caesar left little obvious impression on his famous son. Nevertheless, his death left the fifteen year-old and his two older sisters dangerously exposed.

The task of protecting them now fell on Aurelia's shoulders. With both her husband and her great benefactor, Marius, dead, she had the pressing task of finding her son a suitable wife. Her late husband – with typical lack of ambition – had already arranged a marriage with a relatively low-born woman, but this obviously now needed to be abandoned[17]. The point of patrician marriages was to advance a family's fortunes.

Fortunately, the political calculus of finding a proper daughter-in-law was relatively simple. Since Cinna was in charge of Rome, Cinna's faction must be courted. The wheels of diplomacy duly creaked into motion, and her connections, particularly to the dead Marius, netted a magnificent result. Cornelia, the daughter of Cinna himself, was offered as a bride. What's more, Julius Caesar was made Flamen Dialis – the high priest of Jupiter – an ancient and revered role that came with both a stipend and a modest house. Its many religious restrictions, such as the prohibitions against touching metal, seeing a corpse, or riding a horse, effectively disqualified Caesar from a political or military career, but perhaps that was the point[18]. In such a turbulent world, the priesthood was a stable lifetime career, safely out of the line of fire. Both mother and son should have been well pleased.

There were undoubtedly those who wondered if such a senior role was appropriate for such a young aristocrat. Caesar wasn't much to look at. Now sixteen years old, of moderate height with unnaturally

---

[16] Both Julius Caesar's father and grandfather died this way.

[17] Her name was Cossutia, and there is considerable debate about whether Caesar was married to her or merely engaged. Either way, he would have been fourteen years old when the arrangement took place.

[18] The position of Flamen Dialis predated the Republic and several of its prohibitions were rather odd. For example, Caesar was forbidden from getting undressed outside, naming a dog, touching a bean, or walking under vines.

soft, white skin, he had light, wavy hair, a broad face, and dark eyes. Though not exactly sickly, he was subject to frequent headaches, a condition which would worsen with age, and he frequently seemed on the point of getting sick. His greatest interests appeared to be the latest fashion or gossip, and he spent an inordinate time on his personal appearance. Unlike the more conservative members of his class who preferred a simple toga, he dressed in loose clothes with a belt hanging stylishly around his waist – a look that was soon widely copied by the impressionable youth of the city. There was nothing, in short, to suggest that Caesar was anything more than those with whom he hung around: a rather frivolous dandy. Beneath that weak exterior, however, was an extraordinary self-confidence and an iron will. He was easy to underestimate, but it was dangerous to do so.

If Aurelia had procured the office of Flamen Dialis for her son as a safeguard against future political upheavals, her concerns were quickly proven correct. Hardly more than a year later, Sulla, having successfully concluded his campaign against Mithridates, was once again marching his legions towards Rome. Caesar's new father-in-law, Cinna, was lynched by his own soldiers, and the army that had been sent to stop the invading forces joined them instead. By the time Sulla reached Rome in November of 82 BC, his army had swelled with the addition of more troops including two ambitious young generals named Pompey and Crassus. What was left of Cinna's government collapsed, and a furious Sulla entered Rome. The Caesars had backed the wrong horse.

Marius' entry into Rome had been chaotic and bloody. Sulla's was disciplined and organized – and far worse; as one of his enemies noted, he was at times a lion and at times a fox, but of the two, it was the fox that should be more feared.

What was terrifying wasn't so much the killing, but the way he killed. There was a kind of detached calm to his butchery, almost as if he didn't even consider his victims to be human. His first action upon entering the city was to walk into the Senate chamber and address the assembled patricians. As he was speaking, agonized screams could be heard from the nearby Circus Maximus where his soldiers were busy slaughtering their captives. When the unnerved senators began murmuring, Sulla dryly remarked that he was having a few troublemakers silenced.

Sulla's intention, as he frequently announced, was to fix the broken Republic. The cowed Senate tripped over itself giving him honors. They unanimously voted him the powers of a dictator, the first one appointed in over a century. This was a constitutional position carrying a strict time limit of six months, and always reserved for times of national emergencies. Sulla, however, was given no limits temporal or otherwise to his authority. The self-proclaimed savior of the Republic was a king in all but name.

His first task, as he saw it, was to purge the Senate. He reviewed the senatorial rolls, casually issuing orders to his soldiers to kill those who had been too supportive of Marius and Cinna. After a few days of this, one of his supporters asked the dictator to publish an official list of those he meant to kill in order to spare the rest from nerve-wracking uncertainty. Sulla agreed, and over the next three days a proscription list was published with more than five hundred names on it[19]. The unfortunates who found themselves on the list were to be killed on sight as enemies of the state, with all their property seized or sold at auction. What's more anyone who carried out such a killing would be rewarded with the small fortune of two talents – a sum which could be claimed by anyone, even slaves[20]. As a result, an insidious cloud of fear descended on the city. Neighbor turned on neighbor, friends became suspect, and every social gathering became potentially lethal. Husbands were slaughtered in the sobbing arms of their wives, while mothers had their sons wrenched from their arms and butchered in front of them.

Some of the proscribed were doubtless guilty of supporting the previous regime, but there were many more whose only crime was

---

[19] Although they got their list, it was hardly comforting. After posting it, Sulla unhelpfully announced that it was not exhaustive, but only contained the names that he could think of at that moment.

[20] It's virtually impossible to convert the value of Roman currency to modern equivalents. However, since a talent was originally a unit of weight – usually the mass of water required to fill an amphorae – two Roman talents would be roughly 142 lbs of gold.

being rich. For several months the purge continued, leaving as many as nine thousand dead and a deeply scarred city in its wake.

Somewhat surprisingly, Julius Caesar wasn't one of the casualties. Aurelia's many connections, as well as Caesar's poverty, kept him safe. If anything, Sulla's dictatorship was a blessing in disguise since Caesar was stripped of his priesthood, freeing him up to pursue a military and political career. The only thing required of him was a divorce; one could hardly expect to stay in the dictator's good graces still married to Cinna's daughter. Refusal, of course, would mean only one thing. Sulla was not one to let bygones be bygones. His behaviour upon entering Rome had been dramatic proof of that; one of his very first actions had been to order his soldiers to smash their way into Marius' crypt, drag the rotting corpse through the streets and tear it to pieces.

Divorce shouldn't have been a particularly difficult choice for the eighteen-year-old Caesar. It was an easy price to pay for survival; Cornelia could no longer politically benefit him, and there were plenty of more suitable matches available for an ambitious young man. Caesar, however, was determined to be his own man, and – displaying for the first time that streak of boldness that would carry him to such heights – he refused. It was a grand but suicidal gesture. Caesar's name instantly appeared on the proscription lists and that very night, despite a violent fever, he was forced to flee from Rome.

Chapter 3

EXILE

"The animal known as king is by nature carnivorous"

- Cato the Elder

W hat followed was a harrowing flight that lasted several weeks. He rarely slept in the same spot twice, spending his days in disguise and his nights in damp, uncomfortable holes. The few people who took him in had to be bribed to keep their silence, and his health began to suffer. Sulla's secret police seemed to be everywhere, and on at least one occasion they caught him. While suffering from a debilitating illness – perhaps the first incidence of that sickness that was to shadow his later years – he was arrested, and saved only by a timely bribe to the corrupt captain.

He finally escaped pursuit by joining the army. This was a smart move for many reasons. His chances of a traditional political career were out of reach, but his uncle Marius had already blazed an alternate trail. A military career could easily be parlayed into political office, and the army of the east was safely beyond Sulla's reach. By joining it he could cover himself in glory and return to Rome as a conquering hero.

One of Caesar's first assignments was to visit the court of the elderly Nicomedes IV, the king of Bithynia, in what is today northern Turkey. The kingdom bordered the Black Sea, and Caesar's ostensible mission was to raise a fleet, preferably at Nicomedes' expense. He attacked the job with considerable relish, so charming the old monarch that rumors began to circulate that the two were lovers. His political enemies – of which there would be many – began calling him the 'Queen of Bithynia', a slur which dogged him for the rest of his life. Despite this, the mission was a resounding success, as he persuaded the king to part with most of his fleet[21].

Caesar's reputation was burnished even more when he rejoined the army in an attack on the Greek island of Lesbos. He served there with distinction, winning the civic crown – a chaplet of oak leaves awarded for courage in saving the life of a comrade. This was one of the most prestigious awards that the army could give, and it entitled its wearer to certain preferential treatment. From now on, even senators would have to rise to salute the teenager when he wore it.

While Caesar was in the east beginning his military career, his mother, Aurelia, was busy preparing for his return in Rome. She still had many family connections to prominent Sullan supporters, nearly all of whom were enlisted to beg the dictator to remove her son from the proscription list. Finally, after a badgering campaign culminating with the Vestal Virgins interceding en masse for Caesar, the ageing Sulla relented. Before pardoning him, however, he is said to have snarled that there were "many Marius' in that boy" and that he would ruin them all.

Perhaps wisely, Caesar didn't fully trust Sulla's clemency, and put off returning to Rome for two years until the dictator was safely dead[22]. By then revolution was in the air. One of the year's consuls, a senator by the name of Marcus Lepidus, had raised the standard of revolt, and men – including some of the most famous names in the Senate – were flocking to him. The cronies of the dead dictator were to be swept out of power and the Republic was to be restored to a sound footing.

Caesar hurried to Lepidus' headquarters, where he was welcomed with open arms. Here was the chance that any ambitious young man dreamed of; instant promotion to senior military and political posts

---

[21] The fact that he was still in Bithynia long after he had accomplished this only made the rumors stronger. Whatever their relationship was, it certainly paid off for Rome. When he died six years later, Nicomedes left his kingdom to Rome.

[22] Sulla expired in a fitting fashion. While angrily demanding the strangulation of a corrupt official, he abruptly started bleeding from the mouth and collapsed. He was carried to his bed where he died the next morning.

without the tedious struggle of elections or effort. All he had to do was take hold of the opportunity that was offered.

Julius Caesar – as his later career was to repeatedly prove – was a man willing to take risks, but he wasn't reckless. Lepidus may have had wealth and an army, but he left Caesar cold[23]. Not all the blandishments in the world were worth it if the cause failed, and Lepidus, to Caesar's careful eye, lacked both charisma and talent. All further overtures by the rebel were politely declined.

This turned out to be a wise move. Sulla's government was too entrenched to be so easily dislodged. It also had at its disposal several excellent generals, most prominently the dashing young Pompey. Lepidus' rebellion was easily crushed[24].

Rome was a further disappointment to Caesar; the political atmosphere wasn't nearly as promising as he had been led to believe. The upheavals of the past decade had left the capital with little appetite for revolution, and since Sulla had been remarkably successful in building a stable regime, there seemed little opportunity for a returned exile to carve out a new career.

Sulla had been a strange tyrant; a bloody dictator who sincerely saw himself as the great champion of the Republic. Despite having seized power at the point of a sword, he was no radical. Of ancient patrician stock, he remained at heart an arch-conservative who relentlessly promoted the ancient rights of his class. He recognized that the body politic was sick, and knew both the source of the trouble and its cure. In the old, virtuous days the Senate had guided the Republic to a Mediterranean-spanning greatness. Patrician heroes like Scipio Africanus and Lucius Junius Brutus had defeated would-be-tyrants and barbarian invaders alike. But the past two centuries had seen a slow erosion of senatorial power and prestige as unscrupulous demagogues had increased the power of the plebeians.

---

[23] Lepidus was fantastically rich. He was widely regarded as having the finest house in Rome, complete with a set of ornate bronze shields depicting the fall of Troy. His son and namesake would be one of Caesar's trusted lieutenants and a member of the Second Triumvirate with Augustus.

[24] One of Lepidus' most prestigious supporters was Brutus the Elder, father of the man who would assassinate Caesar. Pompey treacherously murdered Brutus after he had surrendered.

That had allowed execrable 'new men' like Gaius Marius, who lacked both breeding and education, to run roughshod over the constitution. The mob, with its unstable whims and violence, had entered politics, and the entire edifice was now crumbling.

The cure, which Sulla alone had the understanding and tools to implement, was relatively simple. The power of the plebeians must be crushed, and that of the Senate restored. The popular assemblies were duly stripped of their power, and senatorial privileges were vastly increased. Virtually all non-patrician sources of power were neutered, and steps were taken to make the government more orderly. Official ages were set for political offices, and violating the cursus honorum – the usual order of offices – was made a crime punishable by death. Never again would a Gaius Marius hold the consulship seven times.

Or so Sulla had hoped. There was a rich irony in all of this, of course. No amount of finger wagging or senatorial decrees could disguise the fact that Sulla himself had thoroughly violated the Roman constitution. There had been nothing remotely legal about his seizure of power, and – as is usually the case – his example proved far more enduring than his words.

The returning Julius Caesar, now twenty-three, found his political prospects surprisingly undimmed. His military service had marked him as a man of courage, reinforced by the leafy crown he was entitled to wear at all public occasions. Now he needed to attract the attention of the people. Purchasing a modest house in the slum where he had grown up, he offered his services as a public lawyer and cast about for a suitably high profile case.

It didn't take long to find an explosive one. Sulla may have been gone, but his partisans were still firmly in control, and Caesar chose to prosecute two high profile Sullans for corruption. To many it must have appeared as if Caesar had lost his mind and abandoned the good sense he had shown turning down Lepidus, but there were equal parts courage and calculation to his decision. It was one thing to join an armed insurrection led by an incompetent, and quite another to send a personal political message. As always, Caesar bet heavily on himself.

Sulla's cronies were indeed corrupt, and their stranglehold on power was deeply resented by many outside the Senate. The fact that he lost both cases – an inevitability since the Sullans controlled the courts – was beside the point. He had shown that he was willing to risk his life to fight corruption even at the expense of his own class. That identified him as a Populares like his uncle Marius, and made him a darling of the people[25].

It also won him a reputation as a brilliant speaker. Even Cicero, staunch enemy of the Populares, and the greatest orator that Rome ever produced, was impressed. Most people, he grudgingly admitted, couldn't hope to speak so well "even if they gave their lives over to the study of rhetoric."

Caesar's gamble had paid off, but there was still a price to pay: the Sullans weren't amused by the prosecution of two of their own, and a significant chunk of the Senate now detested Caesar as a traitor to his class. Wisely, he announced that he was going abroad, ostensibly to study rhetoric, but in reality to give tempers a chance to cool.

His destination was Rhodes, an island in the eastern Mediterranean which was home to the most famous finishing school in the Roman world. It was run by Apollonius Molon, a master who had taught most of Rome's elite, including Cicero himself[26].

As a diversion from the overheated situation in Rome, the trip was a success, but it was hardly a quiet getaway. He survived the dangerous winter crossing, but was captured by pirates just off the coast of what is today southwestern Turkey. Caesar and his shipmates were taken to the pirates' hidden island base where ransoms were

---

[25] The two "parties" in Rome – the *Populares* and the *Optimates* – weren't political parties in the modern sense. In fact, describing them as political parties can be highly misleading since they both believed that Rome should be governed by the same elite but differed only in their methods. The optimates believed that the traditional manner was best – largely through senatorial deliberation with very limited input from the people. The populares, on the other hand, believed that legislation could be forced through by appealing to the various popular assemblies as well.

[26] In this case, Caesar was literally following in Cicero's footsteps. The great orator, a distant relation of Marius, had dared to convict one of Sulla's proteges a few years before. The dictator wasn't amused and Cicero had – with his usual wit – quickly announced that he was going abroad 'for his health'.

set. The young patrician kept his nerve, assuming an air of breezy superiority that highly amused his captors. When informed that his price was set at twenty talents he haughtily announced that he was worth at least fifty – despite the fact that he was already heavily in debt.

The pirates obliged, more than willing to play his game. Judging from his appearance, he would provide excellent sport. Tall and impeccably dressed in the latest fashion, with his thinning hair carefully arranged to hide the receding hairline, he looked every inch the pompous aristocrat. He stood stiffly, and seemed so vain that he awkwardly scratched his head with one finger to avoid messing it up[27].

It took more than a month for Caesar's agents to raise the funds from the surrounding towns to free him. He found the forced inactivity annoying, since he had kept only his doctor and two valets to share his captivity, sending the rest of his staff after the ransom. To pass the time he composed poetry and read it aloud to his captors who took great delight in telling him exactly how terrible it was. His response was always to call them ignorant barbarians who deserved to be crucified. He would, he assured them, attend to it the moment he was released.

Banter like this amused the pirates, and Caesar kept it up for the entirety of his captivity. It was a strange kind of imprisonment. He participated in athletic contests with his captors, sent them orders to be quiet when he wanted to sleep, and generally behaved as if they were his bodyguards instead of his kidnappers.

Finally, after thirty-eight days, his ransom arrived and Caesar was bid a fond farewell. He was given a guide through the labyrinthine channels out of the pirates' harbor and sent to the nearby Anatolian coast. There, he immediately raised a private fleet, retraced his steps, and caught his former captors completely by surprise. They were taken back to the mainland and – true to his word – crucified to a man.

---

[27] He was inordinately pleased with the Senate's decree to let him wear his oak crown because it hid what he called his "disfigurement".

There was a lesson in all this to a careful observer. Caesar claimed that he bore the pirates no ill will, and as a gesture of mercy had their throats cut before they were nailed to the wood. Personal feelings, however, were beside the point. Even if seemingly spoken in jest, he had given his word to execute them. As all of Rome would soon find out, there was nothing in the world more sacred to the young Julian than his honour. Julius Caesar was not in the habit of making idle boasts.

Chapter 4

THE RISING SUN

"What are laws to those of us with swords?"

- Pompey

The outside world seemed determined to draw Caesar away from his studies. The old rascal Mithridates was once again ravaging Asia, and the war was going badly for Rome. Acting on his own authority, Caesar crossed over to the mainland, raised a private army, and successfully drove out Mithridates' forces. In the process he ensured that the wavering cities of Asia would remain loyal to Rome, and gave the growing number of his partisans in the capital one more thing to boast about. When he returned in 72 B.C., he was easily elected to the post of military tribune – the first rung on the Roman political ladder.

Unfortunately, Caesar's official entry into political life didn't make the splash he had hoped for. While he had been away, the ground had shifted again. Rome was buzzing with the latest exploits of two of its rising stars: Crassus and Pompey. If Caesar's struggles to begin a political career highlighted the dangers of going against the Sullan establishment, theirs illustrated the advantages of courting it.

Marcus Licinius Crassus was perhaps the most calculating man in Rome, and certainly the richest[28]. The son of a famous consul, Crassus had grown up in luxury, but had known poverty as well. His father had been an outspoken supporter of Sulla, and the entire family had paid the price for this gallantry when Marius seized control of the city. The twenty-eight-year-old Marcus had fled to Spain to save his

---

[28] Ironically, he came from the poorer branch of the family. The other one carried the surname *Dives* – "wealthy".

life, his proud father had committed suicide, and the rest of the family was slaughtered.

Crassus' stay in Spain wasn't quite the refuge that he had hoped for. Fear of Marius reached over the Alps, and however sympathetic family friends might be, no one wanted to risk Marius' anger by sheltering an enemy. Crassus, a man who would one day virtually rule the Republic, was reduced to living in a damp Spanish cave.

His fortunes changed eight months later when news of Marius' death reached him, and Crassus immediately began recruiting his father's old allies. He returned to Italy at the head of a modest army, perfectly timing his arrival to coincide with Sulla's attack on Rome. The infusion of fresh troops proved decisive, and the grateful Sulla added him as a close advisor. Having made himself indispensable to the dictator, Crassus had then thrown himself into the task of rebuilding the family fortune.

It was here that Crassus discovered his true gifts. In a world that had no grasp of economics, he was a born capitalist. Although most of his fortune was in real estate, gobbled up cheaply from families that had been ruined in the various wars, he had a hand in almost everything in Rome.

His usual tactic was to buy dilapidated houses, send in an army of highly trained slaves, and turn them into chic apartments which would then be leased out at exorbitant rates. The labourers who improved Crassus' tenements could in turn be rented out to home renovators. Nothing was wasted, and no favour, no matter how insignificant, was ever granted without the expectation of something in return. Within a few years he had built up a real estate empire and network of clients that spread throughout the city. At its height, his personal income rivaled the treasury of the entire Republic. There seemed no limit to his power and influence. As the biographer Plutarch put it, "the greatest part of Rome, at one time or another, came into his hands." The lessons of that lonely Spanish cave had been well learned – he wouldn't be vulnerable and powerless ever again.

Yet this hard-nosed bargaining was leavened by Crassus' undeniable bonhomie. Unlike most Romans of his day he detested florid speeches, and rather democratically refused to look down on any man. There was no citizen too humble, Plutarch informs us, that Crassus wouldn't greet him by name. He was aided in this by a photographic memory, a gift for small talk, and a charming ability to flatter.

He was also undeniably generous. He funded charities, organized a kind of soup kitchen, threw lavish public feasts with enough free grain to feed the entire city for three months, and handed out interest-free loans to put the politically powerful in his debt. All of it, of course, was to increase his stockpile of favors. In first century B.C. Rome everything was for sale, and Crassus had his own ambitions. He once joked – somewhat ominously – that a man shouldn't consider himself rich until he could maintain an army at his own expense.

Political careers in Rome were cripplingly expensive, and Crassus' willingness to extend his bottomless purse gave him a certain popularity. It did not, however, lessen the faint menace that always seemed to cling to him. Not all of his business dealings had been strictly legal, and there were other, darker ways that he had built his fortune. During Sulla's proscriptions he had gained property by adding names to the death lists, and had deliberately ruined at least one Vestal Virgin's reputation to acquire her estate. Perhaps most notorious, however, had been his solution to one of Rome's worst problems.

The elites of the city could afford brick or marble houses, but most of the population lived in cheap, hastily built wooden structures. This made fire, particularly in the poorer areas where the ramshackle buildings were clustered tightly together, a universal and constant fear. Even a slight wind could cause flames to leap from house to house, and once started, the only option was to let a blaze burn itself out. Crassus, with his unerring nose for an opportunity, formed a fire department. When a house caught fire, his representatives would show up, offering to put it out if the owner – and endangered neighbours – would sell their property on the spot for well below the market price. If they refused, he would simply wait, and repeat the offer, this time for significantly less. When the ruined and usually sobbing owners finally sold, Crassus' slaves would extinguish the fire and begin remodelling. Such ruthless dealings left a trail of angry men in his wake. Inevitably, there were rumours that he set some of the fires himself.

For the moment, Crassus was content to wait in the shadows without an overt political agenda. His indisputable power ensured a rare safety; only a fool would want him for an enemy. Young firebrands out to make a name for themselves abused other public figures, but never him. By the time Caesar returned to Rome, Crassus owned a majority of the building contracts in the city, as well as most of the political class. He was a spider at the heart of a vast web which reached into most corners of the city.

But Crassus wasn't the greatest man in Rome. That honor belonged to the city's other rising star, Pompey. Where Crassus had mastered the art of pulling strings in the background, Pompey gloried in the spotlight. He was young, good looking, and always in a rush.

It was this brash urgency which most captured the imagination of his contemporaries. Others may have patiently built up political careers, but Pompey was never one to simply wait his turn. His audacity threw nearly everyone off balance: he seemed to operate as if rules were for lesser men.

Only six years older than Caesar, Pompey had been born into a fabulously wealthy family of the minor nobility. His father was a cross-eyed general known equally for his brutality and flexible loyalties. Although the elder Pompey eventually rose to the rank of Consul, his treacherous behaviour led a contemporary to dub him "the vilest man alive", and his own soldiers refereed to him as "the Butcher". It wasn't a term of endearment. When he died prematurely of the plague, his own soldiers dragged his corpse off its bier and mutilated it.

Young Pompey was an altogether different creature. His boyish looks, perpetually wide eyes and seemingly endless reserve of energy gave him a kind of infectious charm. Those same soldiers who had mangled his father's body followed him willingly, and – with the unruly golden hair dangling over his eyes – soon took to comparing him to Alexander the Great.

Pompey's entire career thus far had been shockingly illegal. Under Roman law a man had to be at least forty and hold the rank of praetor (the second highest magistracy) to command an army. Pompey was barely twenty-two and had never held a political office in his life. With considerable moxie, the young general had offered his services to the ultra-conservative Sulla, the man who was on a crusade to respect tradition. Fortunately for Pompey, the fact that he controlled three legions made up for everything else, and the dictator took the brash young upstart under his wing. He was tasked with clearing Sicily and Africa of Sulla's enemies[29].

This was more than just busy work for a dangerous young general. Sicily and North Africa were the main sources of grain for Rome, and without control of them Sulla's reputation would have been dangerously weakened in the capital. As he was well aware, more than one political career had been undone by rising food prices. This had been a chance for Pompey to show what he could do, and he had taken full opportunity.

Against a far more experienced enemy, Pompey performed magnificently, and with breathtaking speed. In a little over a month he had stormed through Sicily, crushing his opponents with such terrifying ruthlessness that he earned the nickname 'Adulescentulus Carnifex' – Kid Butcher – from his soldiers. When one defeated city demanded mercy, citing an ancient law which protected them, Pompey famously replied, "What are laws to those of us with swords?"[30] His audience was horrified, but he had spoken no more than the current political truth.

North Africa was subdued even faster. Despite taking time off to hunt lions and elephants "so that even the wild beasts would know the courage and strength of the Romans", it took him only forty

---

[29] He was also given the hand of Sulla's stepdaughter in marriage as a sign of the dictator's favour. This started a bitter rivalry with the less handsomely rewarded Crassus who always felt slighted by the endless awards given to his younger rival.

[30] This could serve as an epitaph for his entire career.

days to conquer the entire North African province. He was not yet twenty-four.

The stunning victory only increased Pompey's precociousness. When he returned to Rome, he nearly gave Sulla a fit by demanding a triumph. This was even worse than commanding an army at twenty-three. A triumph was the highest honor a general could receive, the reward for a lifetime of glorious achievement[31]. The triumphant general would ride through the streets of Rome in a gilded chariot pulled by four white horses, dressed in the scarlet robe of Jupiter with his face painted red. Behind would rumble endless wagons of captured treasure, as well as the most impressive of the captives. Innumerable troops, arrayed in glittering dress uniforms, and marching perfectly in sync, would follow behind, a visible symbol of the might of Rome and the popularity of the general. So likely was all this to go to the general's head, that a slave was required to stand beside him, solemnly intoning, "remember, you are just a man".

It was one thing for a grizzled general to be rewarded like this, quite another for a young upstart with no previous record. Sulla, not wanting to be upstaged, had refused permission, and had mockingly greeted him as Pompeius Magnus – Pompey the Great[32].

But Pompey could give as well as he got. He had pointedly refused to disband his army when he reached Rome, and coolly informed the ageing dictator that "men worship the rising, not the setting sun." People had been killed for far less, but Pompey, with all the certainty of youth, had known that time was on his side. Not wishing to risk a civil war, Sulla gave in.

The achievement wasn't lost on Pompey's contemporaries. He became the only person in Roman history to celebrate a triumph without holding political office, and he had done so almost before he could grow a beard. Sulla, however, wasn't completely beaten. The canny dictator granted three successive triumphs – the first to himself,

---

[31] The early Republic's greatest general, Scipio Africanus, was only awarded a single triumph.

[32] Sulla clearly meant this as an insult, but Pompey had the last laugh. He embraced the title and it is as Pompey the Great that he is remembered today.

naturally – and made Pompey go last. The upstart would have his moment, but only after two days of endless parades had glutted the city's appetite.

As it turned out, Pompey's hard-won triumph ended up being somewhat farcical. In order to generate interest, he decided to hitch his chariot to four African elephants instead of the usual horses. Unfortunately, he hadn't thought to check beforehand if elephants could actually fit through the triumphal gate, and the excited crowds who gathered to watch him enter were treated instead to a flustered Pompey attempting to unharness them and shove them through one at a time. Eventually, some acceptable horses were found and the procession continued, but it was hardly the success that Pompey had imagined. Still, for someone who was at least seven years away from being eligible to run for the most junior political office, a triumph was a triumph.

Crassus, of course, had watched all of this with growing exasperation. Whatever pleasure he took from the occasional missteps of Rome's newest wunderkind was blunted by the knowledge that Pompey was succeeding in his bid to become the first man in Rome. Crassus, for all of his careful preparation and immense wealth, was falling further and further behind. As far as popularity went, pulling strings in the shadows couldn't compete with the sight of burnished armour. Fortunately for Crassus, a golden opportunity for military glory was about to present itself.

Chapter 5

INSURRECTION

"Men willingly believe what they wish"

- Caesar

By AD 72, Rome was fighting wars at both ends of the Mediterranean. A revolt in Spain by the last diehard supporters of old Marius had drawn Pompey north in search of more glory, and the seemingly never-ending Mithridatic war was still burning slowly in Asia. It was at this moment, with the Republic militarily overstretched and vulnerable, that a young gladiator named Spartacus escaped from his training grounds and raised a slave revolt.

Gladiator schools were fast becoming the favored producers of entertainment in the Roman world. The steady expansion of the previous two centuries had introduced the Republic to three continents worth of fighting styles, and had added a glut of human chattel to the Republic's busy markets. It helped that many of the slaves had served in various militias, and so already had some rudimentary training. The bloody sand of the arena was the ultimate test of martial skill, a heady attraction in a world where slavery was as ubiquitous as it was unquestioned.

Spartacus was a natural fighter. He had grown up in Thrace, northeast of present-day Macedonia, where he had served as an allied soldier in the Roman army. At some point he deserted, and was captured along with his young wife. He was promptly enslaved and taken to a gladiator school in Capua, about sixteen miles north of modern Naples.

Life as a gladiator wasn't pleasant. The prisoners in Capua were kept in close confinement and seem to have been treated especially cruelly by the master of the school. Spartacus, an intelligent and cultured man, talked nearly two hundred of his fellow slaves into escaping, but was betrayed before he could fully put his plan into action. Realizing that his life was now in jeopardy unless he acted, he managed to break into the dining area, arming his followers with kitchen utensils. In the mêlée that followed, many of his supporters were killed, and fewer than eighty made it to the nearby foothills. There – in a fitting burst of symbolism – they melted down their leg irons into swords.

They had won their freedom, but unless something drastic changed, it was unlikely that they would keep it for long. They had no food or water, no shelter, and no clear objective other than survival. An armed response would soon be on its way – search parties were already being formed – and capture would mean torture, mutilation, and most likely crucifixion. An impromptu vote was hastily taken, and Spartacus was elected as their leader[33].

Their position rapidly improved. Several wagons carrying gladiatorial weapons and armor were seized, and enough wild horses were rounded up to form a cavalry wing. The now heavily armed group relocated to the slopes of Mt. Vesuvius and built a fortified camp. The few local forces that had been sent to find them were easily defeated, and Spartacus began to raid several surrounding towns. This brought in much needed supplies, and effectively solved his manpower problems, as each victory added more runaway slaves to his group.

It also attracted the attention of Rome. Given the ubiquitous way slaves were woven throughout Roman society, revolts – especially ones that were not crushed quickly enough – could easily get out of hand. A grain shortage already had the capital on edge, and the two grinding wars meant that there were few available troops.

There are few records of Caesar's actions during these years, but he probably shared the view of the rest of his class when it came to slaves. Despite the fear of an uprising, slaves were not thought to be particularly effective soldiers. Slavery as an institution was believed to

---

[33] They also chose two slaves from Gaul to form a kind of triumvirate, but Spartacus quickly emerged as the dominant personality.

have a corrupting effect on the enslaved person's morals. Virtues like bravery, honor, and selflessness were eroded, and vices like cruelty, greed, and laziness were increased. Expecting courage from a slave was like expecting compassion from wild animals – it was against their nature. A slave army, therefore, didn't represent the same kind of threat as a foreign one. It lacked discipline and could only be held together by violence. Such mobs might be cunning or vicious, but not tactical or strategic threats. Confirmation of this wasn't hard to find. The last serious uprising had taken place three decades before and – to no one's surprise – had been crushed by the local militia.

The Senate duly appointed one of the year's eight elected praetors, Gaius Claudius Glaber, to the command of a small militia and tasked him with eradicating the threat[34]. Glaber was a reliable choice. A plebeian of no particular distinction or ancestors, he could be counted on to follow standard operating procedures. There would be no foolish heroics or spectacular blunders, just an orderly, methodical campaign that ground Rome's enemies into the dust.

At first, all went according to plan. Spartacus' rabble retreated before Glaber's small force of 3,000 Roman militia, and were soon trapped in their camp with the sheer precipice of Vesuvius behind them. Glaber set up a siege and waited for starvation to do his work for him.

Spartacus, however, refused to follow the script. Instead of tamely waiting for his defeat, he spent his time gathering vines from the surrounding countryside. Fashioning these into primitive ropes, he had his men descend into the dormant volcano under the cover of darkness, climb the other side, and slip behind the unguarded Roman camp. As soon as it was light he attacked, slaughtering virtually everyone.

The Romans stubbornly refused to learn anything from the defeat. It was conveniently chalked up to the unfortunate Glaber's incompetence, and a second militia was dispatched. It suffered the same fate, and this time the lictors – bodyguards of elected officials

---

[34] Praetors were senior magistrates who were authorized to lead armies when the two consuls were otherwise occupied.

and the symbol of their authority – were captured and paraded through the slave camp[35].

This humiliation was a clever touch, demonstrating Spartacus' flair for propaganda. By mocking Rome he dispelled some of the mystique of its name. All through the summer, word of his exploits – and the equitable way he shared his loot – spread, and recruits poured in. Local farmers, resentful of Roman control, brought their horses with them, providing the rebels with cavalry. Each victory, particularly over Roman militia, made the belief that Rome could be successfully defied more real. By the following year, Spartacus' original eighty men had swollen to 70,000.

At last Rome realized the danger it was in. As military tribune, Caesar approved of sending a proper army of 10,000 hardened legionnaires under the command of both consuls to stamp out the rebellion. Marching south, they confronted one of Spartacus' slave generals, killed him and slaughtered 20,000 rebels. The victory confirmed all of the Romans' suspicions about slave armies. Despite their formidable numbers, the rabble would easily be mopped up by proper soldiers. The consuls divided their forces; one blocking Spartacus' escape north, the other running him to ground.

When they finally caught up with him, however, they got a nasty shock. The escaped slaves fought with the desperation of men who had nothing to lose and everything to gain. In two bruising campaigns, Spartacus defeated each consul in turn, proving decisively that properly organized slaves could stand up to the legions.

The victory was seismic, and in typical fashion Spartacus made sure to rub it in. He staged elaborate funeral games for a fallen slave general and forced three hundred of his Roman captives to fight as gladiators. He now had high quality weapons, armor, and an experienced, confident army.

The double consular defeat sent shockwaves of fear and anger through Rome. New generals had to be appointed, but despite the public outcry, there were no volunteers. On the one hand there was fear, but on the other, the risk hardly seemed worth the reward. Even

---

[35] Spartacus ambushed the second militia while its commander was bathing.

if one emerged victorious, a victory over slaves was hardly something to burnish a career. The expense alone was sure to be crippling.

Into the breach stepped Crassus, Rome's most wealthy citizen and a man who knew an opportunity when he saw it. Military accomplishments were what he most conspicuously lacked; here was a first stepping stone to the kind of glory Pompey had, and a chance to be fêted as the savior of Rome. Announcing that he would crush the revolt, he cannily offered to defray the cost of training and equipping a new army as a sign of patriotism. The grateful Senate readily gave him the command, sending him south at the head of six legions – roughly 40,000 men[36].

The approaching Roman army was just one of Spartacus' problems. Ironically, his great victory over the consuls had begun to erode his authority within his own army. It was probably decentralized to begin with – thrown together by necessity rather than inclination – and the confidence gained by defeating the legions made subservience to a single leader less attractive. The original plan seems to have been to escape north and disperse, but now plunder seemed much more attractive. Probably against Spartacus' better judgment the army wheeled south and began to ravage the countryside.

Crassus, meanwhile, seemed in no hurry to get to grips with Spartacus. Most people chalked this up to his methodical nature, but there were also sound military reasons not to rush. It had been more than a decade since he had commanded troops, and if he blundered into some kind of ambush – or worse was outfoxed by Spartacus – the damage to his reputation would be immense. The safest thing to do was to maneuver the slave army into position and then shatter it with a relentless series of hammer blows.

Unfortunately for Crassus, his authority was undercut by questions about his effectiveness as a general. Both legionnaires and officers had understandable doubts about whether a man who had spent the last eleven years building his bank accounts would have the military chops necessary to keep them all from getting killed. There

---

[36] His forces were augmented by the survivors of the two legions that Spartacus had defeated.

would be no outright sedition – Crassus was a very powerful man – but there was a quiet agreement that the more seasoned military minds would act independently if the situation called for it.

This became apparent almost immediately. A subordinate named Memmius was given two legions and ordered to slip behind the slave army while the main force moved into position. Memmius was given strict orders not to engage, but he did anyway and was badly defeated. His two legions suffered heavy casualties and fled back to the main army with nothing accomplished.

Crassus was furious, but was clear-headed enough to realize that part of the failure had been his for not imposing his authority firmly enough. His remedy was to revive the ancient penalty of decimation. The defeated soldiers were divided into groups of ten and made to cast lots. The unlucky man chosen was then beaten to death by the surviving nine in front of the whole army.

The total number of men killed was probably around fifty, but rumor soon ballooned the figure into the thousands. By the time it reached Rome, it was commonly believed that Crassus had decimated the entire army[37]. The lesson was harsh, but it stuck. Crassus was more terrifying than the enemy.

Whatever his soldiers felt about his discipline, there was no arguing with Crassus' results. When one of the various splinter groups of the great slave army – perhaps about ten thousand strong – ran into the Roman army, it was quickly annihilated. Sensing blood, Crassus moved in for the kill.

Spartacus knew that time was running out. After a brief but disastrous attempt to force his way past the encroaching legions, he fled south to the toe of Italy. There he attempted to cross to Sicily to replenish his numbers. But since the slaves had no way of making a fleet, he was forced to make a deal with some pirates to ferry them across. After accepting payment of a large part of the loot Spartacus

---

[37] He had in fact punished every man who fled in typical Crassus fashion- by forcing them to put a down payment on their equipment which would be forfeited if they ran away again.

had collected, the pirates simply sailed away, abandoning him to his fate.

While the slaves were being betrayed, Crassus had trapped them by raising earthworks along the entire thirty-two mile width of the peninsula. Spartacus immediately tried to force his way out, hoping to overwhelm the defenses, but was pushed back with horrendous casualties[38]. Panic began to seize the slaves, and there was talk of surrender. To toughen their resolve, Spartacus crucified a Roman prisoner, and left him screaming for hours, refusing to put him out of his misery. It was an effective warning about the fate that awaited them all if they surrendered or lost. He then began to test the Roman lines, probing with harassing raids to find a weak point.

It wasn't only Spartacus who was feeling the pressure. Despite the fact that Crassus had been in the field for only five months, news of the siege had panicked the Roman government. Sieges were by definition long affairs, and there was no stomach for another one. The war with Spartacus had already been going on for three long years – if Crassus couldn't end it quickly, someone else needed to be appointed to help him. Fortunately, the right person was at hand. Pompey, Rome's greatest general, was on his way back from Spain[39].

This was the worst possible news for Crassus. There was no doubt whatsoever where all the credit would go if the glory-hogging Pompey came anywhere near. To make matters even worse, Spartacus now pulled off a demoralizing act of heroics. Aided by some cavalry reinforcements that had managed to reach him – and a convenient snowstorm – the canny ex-gladiator broke through Crassus' wall.

His moment of triumph was turning into a nightmare. The slave army bolted north, straight toward Pompey, whose veterans would easily slaughter the exhausted mob. Once again, a victory would fall into Pompey's lap, and that swollen head would grow even larger.

---

[38] According to the Roman historian Appian, Spartacus lost twelve thousand men at the cost of three Roman dead and seven wounded.

[39] The Roman historian Plutarch claims that Crassus himself had requested that Pompey be recalled from Spain to assist him. If this is true – an attempt to make his rival into an underling – he quickly regretted it.

Fortunately for Crassus, the slave army instead turned south to confront him. This doesn't seem to have been Spartacus' decision. He was well aware of the danger they were all in and had no illusions of his chances against Crassus in the field. Spartacus' plan seems to have been to try to slip around Pompey's forces and escape across the Alps. His army, however, had other ideas. Pompey was a famous general, battle tested and at the head of grizzled veterans. Far better to face Crassus than the other Roman legions sweeping down on them.

Before the fighting began, Spartacus stabbed his horse to death in front of his men. He was done running. The ensuing battle was both long and bloody, lasting the better part of a day. Spartacus was killed relatively early, cut down as he was attempting to force his way to Crassus. His body was never found. While a few thousand rebels did manage to escape, most of them lay dead on the field at the end of the battle and some six thousand were captured. The slave revolt was over.

Crassus underscored that point by crucifying all six thousand of his prisoners. He started in Capua where the revolt had begun, and every forty yards along the main highway of the Via Appia, nailed a slave to a cross, leaving them to scream in agony. Crassus didn't stop until he reached Rome, covering the entire hundred and twenty miles with crosses. For the many merchants and their accompanying slaves who used the road, there was no way to avert their eyes or cover their ears. The corpses were left there to rot as a ghastly reminder of the penalty of defying Rome.

Chapter 6

THE RIVALS

"Nothing is more unpredictable than the mob, nothing more obscure than public opinion, nothing more deceptive than the whole political system."

- Cicero

C rassus naturally expected a hero's welcome, but instead got a nasty shock. There was rejoicing in the streets of Rome, but the name on everyone's lips was Pompey, not Crassus. On his way back from Spain, Pompey had run into a group of fleeing slaves and slaughtered them. He had immediately written a letter to Rome announcing that while Crassus may have won a battle, he had won the war. Celebrations were announced and the grateful Senate awarded him a triumph. Crassus, meanwhile, had to settle for the less prestigious ovation – a humiliating blow which almost undid the entire point of going to war in the first place[40].

The worst part was that Pompey failed to display even a modicum of embarrassment for stealing Crassus' thunder, and stubbornly refused to share the limelight. This was more than grating. Crassus needed credit for the defeat of Spartacus to ensure his election as consul that year. Pompey, on the other hand, didn't need the glory at all. Beside the fact that he was already famous, at thirty-five he was nearly a decade too young to even run for consul. His grandstanding, therefore, seemed designed specifically to block Crassus' political ambitions.

But when the two victorious generals finally met outside of Rome, it became apparent that Pompey had rather lofty political ambitions

---

[40] Crassus declined the offer to participate in his own ovation by disingenuously suggesting that he had no desire to be honored for defeating slaves.

of his own. A second triumph – an achievement rare enough that even the general who defeated Hannibal hadn't achieved it – wasn't enough. Rules were for lesser men, and nothing less than the supreme office of the Republic was enough. Ominously refusing to disband his army, he demanded to be allowed to stand as consul in the coming election.

The request set off alarm bells within Rome. Neither Crassus nor Pompey had dismissed their troops, and memories of Marius and Sulla were painfully fresh. The bad blood between them was painfully obvious for anyone to see, and questions of which general to back were once again in the air.

To everyone's immense relief, the hand wringing turned out to be unnecessary. The two men met privately and came to an understanding that they would run jointly for the consulship. After a few more days of the tense standoff, Crassus dismissed his army first and publicly offered Pompey his hand in friendship and support.

To outside observers, the two of them seemed genuinely to have buried any hard feelings. Pompey's election was a foregone conclusion – he was the hero of the hour – but he campaigned vigorously for both of them. In one typically excessive outing he made the ridiculous claim that he didn't even want to be consul if he couldn't have Crassus for a colleague. They were elected unopposed, and entered office promising an effective partnership.

There were hopes that this was more than just the usual political posturing. The office of consul was weighty enough that it had sobered its occupants before, and the two men made an intriguing pair. Pompey was popular with the people, but was viewed with suspicion and more than a hint of derision by the blue-bloods of the Senate. He was painfully aware of how they viewed his youth, his humble origins, and his unrefined manners, mocking him the moment his back was turned. Inside Rome, the daring general was transformed into an insecure bumbler. He was so terrified of making some embarrassing *faux pas,* that he had a more experienced friend write up an etiquette script that he could conceal under his toga.

Crassus, on the other hand, wasn't one for the roar of the crowds, but had the impeccable breeding of an aristocrat, and had learned how to make senatorial deals while drinking his mother's milk. If they could put aside their egos, the two of them could dominate Rome; Crassus manipulating the Senate while Pompey dazzled the people.

But behind the scenes, their relationship was not quite so rosy. The two consuls spent the entire time undercutting each other, the result of which was that nothing got done. The Roman system was designed to move slowly, not to grind to a halt. With no major accomplishment to boast about, the joint consulship threatened to turn into a farce. Crassus tried to bolster his flagging popularity with a grand gesture of piety, donating one tenth of his immense wealth to Hercules. Since this included three months of free grain to every citizen and public feasts, it also had the added benefit of making Pompey look stingy by contrast.[41].

Virtually the only significant thing that took place during their consulship was the sensational trial of the governor of Sicily. The defendant, a man named Gaius Verres, was notoriously corrupt, and had ruthlessly plundered the island by – among other things – robbing temples and threatening to crucify those who were too stingy with their bribes. The moment his term of office ended, the furious Sicilians sued him, hiring a rising star named Cicero to plead their case.

Marcus Tullius Cicero was very much a 'new man'. With no prestigious ancestors, vast fortune, or impressive status, he was used to being looked down upon. But his mind was one of the sharpest of his generation – if not all time. He was a magnificent orator and an excellent lawyer, and people came from miles around to hear him speak. Cicero easily won the case and so launched his own political career[42].

---

[41] This was not pure political calculation. Crassus seems to have taken religion seriously, and had previously vowed to make a tithe to Hercules. Unlike most of his peers he had a happy marriage, a scandal-free private life, and was a doting father.

[42] The opposing lawyer didn't even finish the trial. After seeing the effect Cicero's orations were having on everyone, he simply gave up and advised his client to flee.

While Crassus, Pompey, and Cicero were grabbing the headlines, Caesar was laboring up the unglamorous, early rungs of the political ladder. His career so far had been daring, but largely conventional. If anything at all stood out, it was his complete indifference to his mounting debts. The political game was inherently expensive, and Caesar went deeply into debt to fund it. It was almost as if he considered finances unworthy of his attention. Caesar, however, was playing the long game. If going into debt was the way to power, then it was worth the risk.

The trouble, of course, with this strategy was that his family was anything but wealthy, and at some point, the debts would simply overwhelm his ability to pay them back. Examples of this were visible everywhere: Rome was littered with ruined patricians. Ironically, every election Caesar participated in put his future further in jeopardy.

This basic calculus was exacerbated by the relatively low returns that early political investments gave. Election to even a minor post cost a vast sum, and many of the duties while in office had to be funded out of pocket. There was little chance to recoup any of these expenses until a major magistracy was acquired – and several fortunes would already have been spent to get there. The Roman government, for all its democratic tendencies, was essentially restricted to all but the very wealthy.

But these were the rules of the game, and Caesar was interested in power. So, in 69 A.D., he took out yet another loan and somewhat ironically got himself elected to the office of quaestor, a minor position which involved supervising the treasury, as well as a stint assisting the governor of Spain.

Despite the rather colorless job, the year turned out to be a kind of political turning point. For one thing, Caesar's ambition revealed itself in earnest for the first time. Plutarch, who was always on the lookout for a revealing anecdote, informs us that while visiting the Spanish town of Cadiz, Caesar stumbled across a statue of Alexander the Great in the local temple to Hercules. The sight visibly upset him, and when asked why, he responded that at his age Alexander had already conquered the world while he had done nothing worth remembering[43].

The real reason that the year was important, however, was a double tragedy which Caesar brilliantly used to gain a more prominent reputation. The more personal of the two blows was the death of his wife Cornelia. She had been the companion of his youth, married to him for more than a dozen years, and was the mother of his only legitimate child, a daughter named Julia. The cause of her early death is unknown, although childbirth is the usual guess. Either way, few observers expected much grief. Romantic feelings were rarely a part of aristocratic marriages, and Caesar already had a reputation as a womanizer. In a dramatic break from tradition, however, he gave Cornelia a public eulogy. Such things were nearly always reserved for the elderly, or heads of families, and Caesar's delivery therefore, was both shocking and genuinely moving. For the moment at least, his image was recast as that of a loving husband.

All of this was secondary to the main loss that the Julii family suffered with the death of Caesar's aunt, Julia, the widow of the disgraced general Marius. She had been a formidable woman, whose reputation for virtue and devotion to her family had allowed her to keep her wealth and status even during the worst of Sulla's persecutions.

The gambler in Caesar saw an opportunity. Funerals for men of his rank were not just private ceremonies. The procession of mourners would wind through the city, carrying, among other things, wax masks of famous ancestors. This was a moment to show off the family's pedigree, and make an important political statement as well.

Marius was still – nearly twenty years after his death – a lightning rod. If not quite a populist in the modern sense, he had been seen as an opponent of senatorial corruption, and was immensely popular with the common people. Sulla and his cronies had tried their best to change this; all statues of him had been pulled down long ago, and it

---

[43] He was thirty-four, one year older than Alexander ever got. As one commentator put it, this was the age where the two men diverged. For Alexander it marked the end of life, for Caesar, the beginning.

was dangerous to even talk publicly about him. All eyes turned to see what Caesar would do.

His response electrified the city. Flouting the restrictions – and risking a second exile – Caesar marched with the wax mask of Marius prominently displayed for the first time since the old general's death.

The ceremony culminated in an oration by Caesar, which demonstrated his command of the moment. His aunt, he reminded Rome in a brilliant bit of humblebragging, was descended from both royal and divine stock. Her family, therefore, was imbued with the 'sanctity of kings' and was entitled to the 'reverence of gods'. Left unsaid, of course, was the fact that the same blood ran in his veins.

All told, it was a smashing success. His ability to turn tragedy into triumph made him a man to watch, and men like Crassus took notice. The fact that the next year Caesar quietly married Sulla's granddaughter, Pompeia, to ease the fears of those who thought he was too radical only confirmed his political astuteness. Crassus was intrigued. Here was a man who understood the way the world worked. The joint consulship had left Crassus completely eclipsed, but here was a compelling protégée who could be used to bring the spotlight back, and the fact that Caesar was so deeply in debt could only serve Crassus' advantage.

The next decade, however, would belong to only one man. As Pompey had said long ago, men worship the rising sun. Like it or not, Crassus, Caesar, and all of Rome would have to learn to live in Pompey's shadow.

Chapter 7

THE AGE OF POMPEY

"He seemed... to have led the whole world captive"

- Plutarch

By 67 B.C., Pompey was listless, frustrated, and generally miserable. His consulship had made it clear that he would never be at home in Rome. The Senate was full of jackals, vicious beasts who would just as soon knife a man as smile at him. The fact that they were also insignificant mediocrities who constantly snubbed him only made it worse. He desperately wanted to get away. He was a man of action, and he needed fresh air, the command of men who did what they were told, and the glory of the battlefield. Fortunately for Pompey, there was a military crisis freshly available.

The Roman world had always had a problem with pirates – Julius Caesar could vouch for that – but in the 60's things had gotten completely out of hand. The eastern wars with Mithridates had displaced large numbers of soldiers who had turned to piracy as an easy way to make a living. There were always places to hide in the gaps between civilization, and in the absence of any effective police force it was virtually impossible to root them out.

The area known in antiquity as Rough Cilicia – the coast of what is now southern Turkey – formed the heart of a virtual pirate kingdom. Safe amid the countless caves, harbors and hideouts that dotted the eastern Mediterranean, the pirates began to mobilize whole fleets and expand outwards. By 67, they controlled over four hundred coastal towns and were raiding Roman shipping with impunity. Instead of concealing their activities, they began to flaunt them. Pirate ships now boasted gilded masts, purple sails, and silver-plated oars.

The new wealth also underscored Rome's impotence. The pirates were untouchable, and they knew it. They seemed almost sadistically determined to humiliate the Republic. If a Roman citizen was discovered among their prisoners they would pretend to be terrified, and grovel at their prisoner's feet. After begging forgiveness they would dress them in a toga, invite them to swim home, and shove them overboard.

It wasn't long before Italy itself came under attack. Unsatisfied with the relatively easy coastal targets, pirate raiding parties began to travel inland to sack the grand summer villas of the rich. Even worse, they started to kidnap Roman officials. When an ex-consul was assigned the task of dealing with the issue, his daughter was abducted, as were two praetors in full regalia – lictors and all[44]. Most humiliating, however, was a pirate attack on the Roman fleet itself while it sat at anchor. Rome's port was set on fire, the fleet was destroyed, and yet more hostages were taken.

This was the final straw, not just because of the embarrassment, but because the pirate's activities had severely impacted Rome's grain supply. The capital imported most of its grain from Sicily, and as the pirates grew more bold, grain prices began to steadily climb. The destruction of the fleet coincided with a famine which made starvation a real possibility. Something clearly had to be done. The pirates now had Rome's full attention.

A tribune in Pompey's pay floated the idea of granting Pompey special powers to deal with the situation. This was sensible enough, but the scope of the suggested authority was enough to catch the breath. Pompey would be granted imperium infinitum – power not restricted to a single province, but over the entire Mediterranean, its islands, and fifty miles inland. He would outrank every government official, commander, senator, or consul, and would keep this status for three years or until the crisis ended – whichever came first. In

---

[44] The ex-consul was an ancestor of the future triumvir Mark Antony. The fate of the kidnapped is unknown, although slavery was the most likely result since pirates were the main supplier of slaves to the Mediterranean world. By 67 BC more than 10,000 were being sold per day in the slave markets of Delos.

addition, he would be tasked with overseeing Rome's grain supply for five years.

This was more power than any Roman had ever had in peacetime. It effectively suspended the constitution and made Pompey a dictator, allowing him to control the supply of food to the capital, and with it the urban mob. The senatorial horror that greeted this proposal must have delighted him almost as much as the roar of the crowds.

The Senate tried to block the measure, but Pompey's agents had now whipped up the mob, and the people were in no mood to be denied[45]. Violence on both sides erupted, but in the end Pompey got what he wanted.Julius Caesar, as always taking the pulse, was one of Pompey's more vocal supporters in the Senate. Pompey was a king in all but name, personally in charge of five hundred ships, one hundred and twenty-five thousand men, and a vast war chest. No doubt grinning from ear to ear, he left Rome in triumph.

Now Pompey had to deliver. The day after his appointment, the price of grain fell in anticipation of his success, which ratcheted up the pressure. Piracy was a problem that had never been solved in the ancient world; he had three years to do the impossible.

Fortunately, it was a crisis perfectly suited to his skills. He was not a deep thinker or a particularly original strategist, but he was a brilliant administrator. The entire Mediterranean was divided into twenty-four tidy sections, each under the authority of one of his sub-commanders and supported by infantry on the coasts. Starting at the western end, he used his fleet like a great broom – in his words – to sweep the pirates east into designated killing zones.

In forty days he had the pirates bottled up in Rough Cilicia, and was in position to besiege their main citadel. Rather than wait for starvation to do the trick he stormed it, capturing some twenty thousand men, ninety ships and a massive amount of loot. Normally the captured pirates would have been crucified or sold into slavery, but Pompey rather shrewdly settled them in depopulated areas of Asia

---

[45] According to Plutarch, when one tribune tried to veto the proposal, the angry roar of the crowd was loud enough to kill a raven flying overhead.

Minor and Greece instead[46]. This worked out surprisingly well for everyone. Many of the able-bodied men he captured had turned to piracy to escape poverty, and giving them land solved that problem honestly. Pompey's settlement, therefore, was more permanent than the usual scare tactics could hope for. Even better for Pompey, those newly established landowners were now clients of his, giving him yet another power base in the southern Mediterranean[47].

The satisfied general announced his intentions to return to Rome and relinquish his unusual powers to bask in the adulation of the masses. Even his most bitter political enemy had to admit that Pompey had done something extraordinary. In less than three months he had solved an issue that had plagued the Mediterranean world for centuries, and he had done so without abusing his immense authority.

But Pompey wasn't quite finished. The campaign had gotten his blood up and he had no desire to return to his cage in Rome just yet. One of the reasons that the pirates had been such a problem recently was that they were getting aid from – and aiding – that old rascal Mithridates. Defeating him once and for all would be a crowning glory in Pompey's career.

The fact that the Poison King was even still around causing trouble was a minor miracle in itself. He was now in his third war – in as many decades – with Rome. He had made a career out of annoying the Roman state, never winning, but somehow slipping away each time with his kingdom intact.

There was already a commander named Licinius Lucullus in the field against Mithridates, but it was easy enough for Pompey to have him fired and take up the command himself. Lucullus protested furiously, but there was nothing he could do. The fact that his men universally sided with the exciting Pompey, further soured his mood. For Caesar, watching from Rome, this was a salutary lesson that he would never forget. Everything rested on the loyalty of the men.

---

[46] He also founded a city on the Black Sea – called Pompeiopolis naturally – and relocated some of them there.

[47] He had done the same thing in Spain after winning the war against Marius' supporters.

Once in command, Pompey moved quickly. Instead of attacking Mithridates directly, he went after his allies, systematically removing them from power.[48]. Within three years, Rome's old enemy had committed suicide[49]. When news reached the capital, the streets exploded with demonstrations in support of Pompey. A grateful Senate declared ten successive days of celebration.

Pompey, however, wasn't quite finished. As with the pirates, he was interested in a permanent settlement, so he had decided – on his own initiative – to reorganize the entire East. Existing kingdoms, some of which had been established by Alexander the Great, were swept away or made subservient to Rome, and new provinces were created with Pompey's clients in control. Bureaucracies were streamlined, tax collection was organized, and trade deals were hammered out[50].

When these arrangements were complete, Pompey was finally ready to return home. He was – as he was perfectly aware – the greatest Roman who had ever lived. He had stamped his name on three continents, an accomplishment which not even Alexander the Great could equal, and his client list included princes, kings, and even whole provinces.

He had never considered modesty a virtue, but now there was no longer a need to even pretend. He was returning to the capital a god among men. He had made treaties, established provinces, and annexed territory – all without even the pretence of consulting the senatorial pygmies back home. As far as he was concerned, the only mistake that Rome had made was to deny him a crown.

Now the king was coming home.

---

[48] The most important ally was his son-in-law Tigranes, who ruled a neighbouring kingdom. Tigranes, who made it a point never to appear in public without at least four subject kings in attendance, surrendered almost immediately in exchange for keeping his throne.

[49] Ironically, Mithridates, the Poison King, tried to poison himself. After repeated attempts failed, he had a bodyguard dispatch him.

[50] Pompey mortally offended the Jews by entering the inner sanctum of the Temple, and was surprised to find it largely empty. The local he left in charge – an Edomite named Antipater – was the father of Herod the Great who ruled Judea when Jesus Christ was born.

Chapter 8

CATILINE

"If you must break the law, do it to seize power: in all other cases observe it."

- Caesar

I n Pompey's absence, Julius Caesar had been slowly making his way up the political ladder. In 66 he had been appointed surveyor of one of Rome's most important roads[51], and the next year he had been elected aedile, a position that oversaw the markets, public buildings, and several official celebrations in Rome. Both of these elections had been bankrolled by Crassus, which was fortunate, since Caesar's finances were now alarmingly bad.

The funding was a part of Crassus' increasingly desperate bid to stop Pompey. Ever since his rival had left to deal with the pirates, Crassus had been scheming to undermine, or at least restrict his power. On one occasion he had even proposed invading Egypt – a current ally – so the Senate would have a counterbalance to Pompey's growing client list. All of these attempts failed, however, and it seemed that the more Crassus tried to weaken him, the more popular Pompey got.

Crassus' new strategy, therefore, had been to build up his power in the Senate where he could outsource the job to promising young senators. Caesar was the ideal candidate for this. He was ambitious, clearly talented, and most importantly, massively in debt.

Among other things, the job of aedile involved maintaining public buildings, cleaning roads and sewers, and ensuring that the city's grain supply was secure – hardly tasks to quicken the pulse. Caesar, of course, found a way to make even these mundane tasks

---

[51] The Appian Way – still in use today.

exciting. Under the guise of preserving public structures he restored all the statues of Marius that had been taken down by Sulla. Cleverly, he made this divisive act look like an act of healing by publicly pointing out that both Marius and Sulla were citizens of the same Republic.

The real advantage of being aedile, however, was in their function of hosting public games. The state offered a modest allowance to pay for these, but to make them truly memorable, it was necessary for the aedile to dip into his own pockets. The good will gained from an impressive show could fuel a quick rise to higher office, while a disappointing one could derail a political career. In practice this meant that every aedile had to outdo the previous one, which in turn meant astronomical sums had to be spent.

Caesar, who always seemed completely indifferent to his debts, threw himself into the challenge. Temporary columns were set up to transform the Forum, and the space was filled – along with the buildings surrounding it – with priceless works from his private art collection. Exotic beasts from three continents were brought to Rome, and since there were no permanent amphitheaters, a temporary one was set up to exhibit them.

The final stroke was a series of gladiatorial shows. This was an unusual addition because gladiator fights were exclusively reserved for funerals. To get around this restriction, Caesar announced that he was staging them as a tribute to his father who had died nearly twenty years before. Caesar, of course, didn't do anything half-heartedly, and the scale of his plans unnerved the Senate. He hired so many gladiators that some senators began to wonder what his real aims were. It had only been six years since Spartacus had died, and the thought of so many heavily armed men in the city – under the control of one man – set off alarm bells. Before Caesar could start his games, a bill was rushed through that limited the number of gladiators that could be displayed at one time.

In the end it hardly mattered. The reduced number – three hundred and twenty gladiators, all of them decked out in ceremonial silver armor – delighted the crowd, and made Caesar the celebrity of the day.

Caesar may have considered the cachet acquired with the people to have been worth the new debt, but those around him weren't so sure. Before he had even started his first political campaign he was already thirty one million sestertii in debt and this latest spending spree at least doubled that[52]. The path to political power was a kind of golden straitjacket. In order to pay his bills, and keep the loans coming, Caesar had to have a political future – or at least the appearance of one – that was lucrative enough to make it worth the risk. That meant taking greater risks himself. Two years later he ran for the post of Pontifex Maximus – the chief priest of the Roman religion. Defeat would mean political and financial ruin, for himself and his entire family. As he left his house on the morning of the election he told his mother that she would see him return as Pontifex Maximus – or not at all.

Debt had pushed more than one man inexorably to revolution. The prime example was Sergius Catiline, who was tried for corruption while Caesar was overseeing the courts. Like Caesar, Catiline was a member of an old family that had become impoverished and was seemingly in terminal decline. There, however, the comparison stopped. Catiline got a lucky break by backing Sulla in the civil war, and had managed to launch a political career through the contacts of the dictator[53]. His limited resources, however, couldn't keep pace with his ambitions. A minor governorship in Africa where he spent his time extracting vast sums of money by thoroughly illegal means seemed to solve his financial issues, but the resulting extortion charges dragged on and on, eating up most of his ill-gotten gains[54].

As if this wasn't enough, in 64 BC, a new quaestor named Cato, whose personal mission in life seemed to be to fight corruption and return the Republic to the old manly virtues it had been founded on,

---

[52] Thirty one million sestertii equalled about 1,300 talents. Since the sestertius was made of copper, that would equal 92,300 pounds of copper.
[53] Pompey, Cicero, and Catiline all served together in Sulla's army.
[54] Ironically, as it turned out, Cicero offered to defend him, but the proud Catiline refused his services. His debt, made worse by his taste for excess, drew him into increasingly more bizarre plots. In one instance he supposedly planned to kill the sitting consuls and install himself as dictator.

insisted on digging up the names and punishing all those who had profited during Sulla's proscriptions.

Catiline was duly tried for murder, a crime of which he was obviously guilty. In the days after Sulla's takeover, he had killed his brother-in-law and then paraded through the streets waving the bloody head. More recently, it was whispered that he had murdered his own wife and son because a well-connected mistress refused to have a relationship with a married father.

Guilt and a guilty verdict, however, weren't the same thing. Catiline's remaining resources were deployed – favors were dispensed, bribes were handed out, and promises were made. In the end, to nobody's particular surprise, he was acquitted, wriggling free yet again.

This presented something of a problem for Caesar, whose job it was to ensure that the courts functioned properly. Earlier that year he had convicted Catiline's uncle of the same crime, and there was no doubt at all that Catiline should have been convicted. But Catiline was also a mutual client of Crassus, and increasingly popular with the people who saw him as a champion of those in debt. There was much more to be gained by letting him go free. Caesar let the acquittal stand.

It was the smart political move, but it had serious repercussions. Catiline's crushing debts remained, and the only chance to escape them was to be elected consul. In the most bitterly contested campaign in recent memory, he ran as a radical populist, promising to cancel all debts. This made him wildly popular with the poor, but – since most of the creditors were senators – it made him equally unpopular with the aristocracy.

Thanks to aristocratic resistance and his unsavoury reputation, Catiline's bid for consul failed. To add insult to injury, he came in third behind a nonentity and Cicero, a new man without prestigious or even aristocratic ancestors. Catiline's political hopes were ruined. There was no way out, no escape. The only choice left was to overthrow the Republic.

Caesar may not have been reckless enough to join Catiline, but he could certainly sympathize. His own debts were well known, and it wouldn't take much for him to end up in the same position. In any case, there was plenty of quiet support from senators in similar straits, and Catiline began to stockpile weapons and search for allies in the towns of Italy.

To allay suspicion, he continued to attend the Senate, but this proved to be a costly mistake. Before he was ready to act, his mistress betrayed the plot to Cicero who proceeded to deliver a fiery series of orations, excoriating the disgraced patrician. Catiline angrily defended himself, mocking the Senate for putting their trust in a commoner like Cicero. That very night, however, Catiline fled to his waiting troops, conspicuously donning the robes of a consul along the way.

Rome was gripped with a nervous excitement as reports of a countryside in flames began to trickle in. Neither consul had anything approaching a distinguished – or even competent – military career, and there was no obvious alternative close to hand. Julius Caesar argued that Pompey should be recalled from the east to deal with the situation, which was both a subtle insult to the current consuls and a clever way to ingratiate himself with the most powerful man in the Roman world[55]. The measure was vetoed and rioting broke out in the streets. Why, the mob asked, wouldn't the Senate call its greatest general?

Caesar had adroitly used the brewing crisis to put himself in the spotlight, but his new status as Pompey's spokesman backfired almost immediately. As the violence spun out of control, the protestors roaring for Pompey's recall began to look more menacing than the distant Catiline, and opinion began to turn against Pompey. The tribune who had been Pompey's most vocal champion, lost his nerve and fled to the general, making the entire episode look like an attempted coup. Caesar now appeared to be a dangerous rebel, and the Senate immediately suspended him. Realizing his mistake, he wisely accepted the punishment, and retired calmly to his house. The next morning an angry mob gathered outside his front door, intent on restoring him to office by force, but, correctly judging the mood of the city, he told them to disperse instead. Impressed by his restraint,

---

[55] One can only wonder what his patron Crassus thought of this.

the Senate promptly reinstated him. The rule of law had triumphed over the passions of the crowd. Pompey would stay in the East.

This was Cicero's moment. The Senate passed its consultum ultimum – a bill granting him the authority to deal with the crisis in a manner that he saw fit. The next day he produced incriminating letters and arrested five conspirators who were still in the city. Acting quickly under the authority he had been given, he declared them guilty and proposed that they should be condemned to death without a trial.

Virtually the only voice raised in dissent was Caesar, who – in what would be a lifelong pattern – argued for clemency, pointing out that the accused were all Roman citizens. Depriving them of their right to defend themselves in a trial might have drastic consequences in the future. If they really wanted to punish the guilty, why not consider permanent imprisonment where they could spend a lifetime paying for their crimes[56]? At the very least, why not wait until passions had cooled before deciding their fate?

He spoke so eloquently that most of the senators switched sides, and it looked as if leniency would carry the day. Cicero, however, spoke next, and his words worked their usual magic. His speech was followed up by a rousing oration by the inflexible quaestor Cato, after which the senators voted overwhelmingly for the death penalty.

Caesar's request for mercy showed considerable bravery. More than one senator noted darkly that he had been on friendly terms with the disgraced rebel. To ask for clemency for a traitor who had been caught in the act seemed to many to be a tacit admission of guilt. Tempers got so heated that some young senators and knights drew their swords and would have killed Caesar if Cicero hadn't called them off. Caesar was forced to avoid the Senate House for the next few days until tensions had cooled[57].

---

[56] Life imprisonment, though common in the modern world, was a novel suggestion in Caesar's day.

[57] Crassus was suspected of having a hand in Catiline's conspiracy as well, but most people were smart enough to keep those thoughts to themselves. When one firebrand had the audacity to openly accuse him, he was shouted down. A few days later the man was quietly murdered.

The most serious repercussion of the trial for Caesar was the new enemy he gained. During the debate, Cato, who was quickly earning a reputation as a moral crusader, relentlessly attacked Caesar. The more Caesar calmly responded, the angrier and more insulting Cato grew. At the height of their exchange, one of Caesar's slaves brought in a note and handed it to him. Cato, suspecting that this was a secret communication with Catiline's rebels, demanded that the note be read publicly. When Caesar refused, the surrounding senators shouted their approval and Cato triumphantly demanded it again. Caesar calmly handed it over, and Cato was horrified to discover that it was a love letter from his own sister, Servillia, requesting a tryst with Caesar. From that moment Cato was a lifelong enemy of Caesar[58].

The risk of asking for mercy for Catiline, however, was worth it to Caesar. The mob loved Catiline – or at least his idea of debt forgiveness – and Caesar had come as close as he could to showing sympathy. He had shown conclusively that he was still the people's champion in the Senate.

Fortunately for everyone, Catiline's revolt fizzled out almost before it began. His troops were ill-armed and disorganized, unnerved by Cicero's quick action. Two thirds of them simply deserted when the plot was uncovered, and those that remained proved no match for the legions.

The struggle was short and bloody. Catiline was one of the first to die, falling, as one writer reported, far ahead of his men. In Rome, Cicero was hailed as the savior of the Republic. He was escorted by torchlight through the city, and his grateful colleagues voted him the title Pater Patriae – the father of his country.

The praise went completely to Cicero's head. He composed a long poem about himself, and spared no occasion to remind everyone of his bravery and decisiveness[59]. His enemies, of which there were

---

[58] The two families would remain enmeshed. Servillia was the mother of Brutus, Caesar's most famous assassin.

[59] Even Cicero's most bitter enemy admitted that he was a brilliant speaker and writer. His poetic attempts, on the other hand, were universally agreed to be atrocious. Perhaps mercifully, therefore, the poem to himself has not survived.

many, countered by pointing out that he had illegally executed Roman citizens. From that moment on, he was constantly under threat of prosecution and exile – a strange end to what had been a triumphant consulship.

Cicero's fate was typical of Rome, and a warning for Caesar. In the jostle for power, the only thing that united everyone was jealousy of those who rose too quickly or too high. Ambitious men had to be cut down to size before they became a threat. The result was a city of pygmies, eternally fighting for supremacy. Rome was a cesspool; morally corrupt, scandal-ridden, and deeply divided. Nothing improved, nothing got done, and the only changes seemed to be worse ones. The city was in desperate need of a savior.

To Caesar's eyes, the only hope of escaping the endless cycle of squabbling, was to follow the footsteps of Marius and Sulla. They had gained towering reputations by winning battles abroad, and then had returned to Rome to impose their will on everyone else.

Now history seemed poised to repeat itself. As the year 63 drew to a close, and Caesar contemplated his next steps, news came from the east that a new Sulla was on his way. Pompey was coming home.

Chapter 9

THE RETURN OF THE KING

"Lightning always strikes the tallest trees"

- Herodotus

Caesar had good reason to feel ambivalent about Pompey's return. His debts were growing ever greater, and the only thing keeping his creditors at bay was the potential of further political success. Even if Pompey didn't decide to make himself dictator – and there was nothing really to stop him – his mere presence in the city would suck up all the oxygen. Advancement would be through his good graces, and if he took a dislike to Caesar – or worse, viewed him as a threat – that would effectively end Caesar's career[60].

This was all the more frustrating, because that year had seen his political career start to take off. His election to Pontifex Maximus had been hotly contested, but in the end, he had won a landslide victory. The new job came with a nice salary, and, more importantly, a large house in the center of the city. He had always lived in the Subura, an unfashionable district in one of the poorer neighborhoods of Rome. Caesar had, of course, put the optics of this to good use, but now that his credentials as a man of the people were established, it was no longer necessary. The new home was located on the eastern end of the Forum, close to the political heart of the city.

On one level it was strange that Caesar was now the chief priest of the state religion. He was privately skeptical of the gods, and rarely invoked them publicly, except to say that he was blessed by luck. This didn't have the somewhat negative connotation that it does for us – as

---

[60] Caesar, a notorious womanizer, had taken advantage of Pompey's absence to have an affair with his wife.

if he were not talented but merely lucky. He meant that he was a favorite of the goddess Fortuna, more often the recipient of her favors than her cruel whims. But he also believed that a lucky break had to be followed up by hard work. Fortune might present an opportunity, but it was up to you to grasp it at the right moment. As he told his soldiers, "If things don't go as they should, we must help fortune by efforts of our own".

In one other way it had been an important year, although he certainly didn't know how much at the time. His niece Atia gave birth to a son, and Caesar, as head of the family, travelled to a small city to the south of Rome, to congratulate her in person. There he met his grand-nephew, Gaius Octavius, the future emperor Augustus, for the first time.

Caesar, along with all of Rome, braced himself for Pompey's return, and the victorious general didn't disappoint. Triumphs by nature were designed to overawe the populace, and Pompey was in a mood to boast. Months had been spent in preparation for this moment, and it had probably occupied his thoughts to some degree throughout his time in the East. He was now by far the richest man in the Republic, outstripping even Crassus' wealth, and he poured his resources into the display[61].

All of the usual highlights were there – the endless food and wine, gold and silver trophies, long lines of captives, and glittering columns of troops. Some of the soldiers carried huge placards inscribed with the names of nations that he had conquered, others carried lists of his accomplishments: twelve million enemies vanquished, a thousand fortifications stormed, nine hundred cities captured along with eight hundred pirate ships, and the building of at least thirty-nine cities. Other soldiers carried huge paintings showing pivotal episodes of Pompey's various wars, or posters proclaiming how much each soldier gained in loot – more than ten years' pay. There were so many exotic

---

[61] The wealth he brought back with him is nearly incalculable. Some estimates put just the gold at 40,000 talents. He almost tripled the annual income of the entire Republic.

animals, grand prisoners, and sheer treasure hauled in that it took two full days to complete[62].

The grand finale – carefully timed to be on his forty-fifth birthday – was a team of horses pulling a massive portrait bust of Pompey made entirely out of pearls. Behind it, riding in a chariot heavily encrusted with gems, rode the great man himself. Tradition dictated that the triumphing general wear a gold embroidered, purple robe, but Pompey instead sported a bright red one that had once belonged to Alexander the Great[63].

The message could hardly be missed. Pompey, with his shock of still- blond hair, was a new Alexander. He had triumphed on all three continents of the world, and had returned from the east something more than mortal. As the writer Plutarch put it, "he seemed...to have led the whole world captive".

It was what came next that terrified everybody. Pompey had nearly forty-five thousand soldiers at his disposal and a limitless supply of wealth. There was no one in Rome – or anywhere else – that was strong enough to oppose him. With the sound of hobnailed boots still ringing through the streets, there was no one who would even dare to contradict him. Would he tamely dismiss his soldiers, give up all that immense power, and take up the mundane lifestyle of a civilian? Or had his time in the east given him a taste for monarchy?

If recent history was any guide, the answer was obvious enough. Sulla had had far less power when he forced himself on Rome, and it was an open secret what Pompey thought of the capital. After the Senate had balked at one of his proposals, one of his subordinates had ominously written, "what is the Senate that it should hobble the tamer of the world?"

Pompey had made it quite clear what he wanted: official ratification of his settlement in the East and – more importantly – land to give to his veterans. Both of these could have been easily accomplished with a little show of force, but Pompey surprised

---

[62] Among Pompey's captives were princes, princesses, queens, and two kings, all wearing their national costumes.

[63] He had found it among the personal belongings of Mithridates after the latter's suicide.

everyone by dismissing his troops, and quietly taking his seat in the Senate instead.

It was a magnanimous gesture by a man whose reputation was so great that he had no need for petty thuggery. The entire city hung on his every word or gesture, what need did he have for swords when even the Senate was desperate to please him?

Unfortunately for Pompey, he had seriously miscalculated in two ways. The first was in assuming that the respect he was given was for anything other than the nine legions he controlled. The second was in overrating his own political skills.

Every Roman who rose high enough got their wings clipped. There were no exceptions other than Sulla who had died before he could suffer the common fate. This was the crucial unwritten rule of politics: greatness was revered, but excessive greatness was hated. "Lightning", as the Greeks said, "always strikes the tallest trees". No one person could be bigger than Rome.

Before Pompey even returned to the capital, an anti-Pompey group had been forming. Chief among them, of course, was his old rival Crassus, but the true leader was Marcus Porcius Cato the Younger.

Of all the figures in the waning days of the Republic, Cato seems the strangest to modern eyes. As stubborn as a mule, he was utterly charmless, allergic to compromise, and seemed devoid of even the slightest trace of warmth. These very traits, however, were what endeared him to the Roman people. He was utterly incorruptible, brutally honest, and had a will that was every bit as strong as Caesar's. His uncompromising stands were seen by his contemporaries – with a mixture of awe and fear – as something out of the ancient past[64]. He was a living reminder of the values that had made Rome the master of the classical world.

The Roman government was designed with a conveniently large number of ways to thwart actions the Senate disapproved of,

---

[64] His great grandfather, Cato the Elder, had been famous for his virtue, particularly in upholding pure Roman values in the face of the corrupting influences of the Greek east.

and Pompey's enemies exploited all of them to frustrate him. His eastern settlements were delayed again and again, as were his more pressing calls for land to settle his veterans. Pompey, so confident on the battlefield, seemed utterly bewildered by politics. With frustration came the dawning realization that disbanding his troops had been a mistake. The senators may have applauded the laying down of his arms, but that hadn't brought the respect he so desperately craved. It had actually accomplished the opposite. Without his soldiers, he was just another retired general. Much of the fear that had surrounded him dissipated, and with it the deference to his wishes. As a young man in Africa he had quipped 'what are laws to those of us with swords?' That had always been his problem. He responded to obstacles with frontal assaults. But what was Pompey without a sword?

The general's frustrations were a godsend for Caesar. The political stage was crowded, and Pompey's diminishment made room for everyone else. Caesar managed to keep his name on everyone's lips with the aid of a sensational trial which completely absorbed Rome's attention.

Caesar was already a well-known womanizer. His list of conquests – according to rumors – included many of the city's most prominent wives, who found his mix of charisma and wit irresistible. Sometimes the husbands took this in their stride – neither Pompey nor Crassus seem to have objected when Caesar seduced their wives – but for others it was salt rubbed into a wound. This made it particularly delicious when a scandal erupted involving Caesar's wife, Pompeia. For once, the shoe was on the other foot.

As Pontifex Maximus, Caesar's house was used to celebrate the festival of the Bona Dea, a solemn, female-only celebration that took place in May and December. Since all males, including animals, were explicitly forbidden, Caesar left for the night, leaving his wife Pompeia, and his mother, Aurelia to host.

This absence provided a perfect opportunity for a wild aristocrat named Publius Clodius Pulcher to attempt to seduce Pompeia. Clodius was a darling of the mob who already had a long history of mischief.[65]. He was the youngest son of a branch of Rome's most ancient family, the Claudians, who were as unstable as they were glamorous. Clodius had inherited the family traits in full. He was good looking, charismatic, and completely unprincipled.

His plan wasn't particularly subtle. Since it was a female-only occasion, he put on some women's clothes, grabbed a lute, and walked through the open front door. Unfortunately, he got lost trying to find Pompeia, and was discovered almost immediately. Pandemonium erupted, and in the chaos he managed to sprint outside with the screaming women in hot pursuit.

The stunt managed to offend nearly every sober person in Rome. Never in Rome's long history had the Bona Dea ceremony been profaned. Caesar immediately divorced Pompeia, and Clodius – who belatedly realized that he had gone too far – was tried for sacrilege. Clodius' ridiculous defense – that he hadn't been in Rome that day – was easily destroyed by Cicero, who had actually met with him on the day in question. Cicero's testimony to that effect destroyed the defendant's case. Clodius never forgave him.

Caesar was called as a witness, but refused to testify, claiming that he had no idea if Clodius was guilty. When asked why he had divorced his wife then, Caesar famously responded, "because Caesar's wife must be above suspicion".

It made for a nice quote, another example of Caesar's all-consuming pursuit of reputation. Perhaps he really did think this way, or maybe it was just a convenient excuse to get out of his marriage. The union with Pompeia had been purely political – she was from a safely conservative family at a time when he was trying to reassure the conservatives – but they lacked the connections he needed to advance his career. In any case, Clodius still remained popular with the mob, and Caesar had no wish to antagonize them by testifying. His political instincts, as usual, proved correct. Clodius'

---

[65] He was born with the name Publius "Claudius", but later in life changed it to "Clodius" as a political stunt. Since it is as Clodius that he is known to history I've only referred to him by that name.

family was rich enough to secure a not-guilty verdict, and he emerged from the trial as a minor celebrity[66].

By the time the verdict was formally announced, Caesar had left Rome. His debts had finally caught up with him. Caesar had finally been awarded the governorship of a province – this time Spain – and he had begun making plans for his departure. However, the province was comparatively poor when compared to others which suggested that the likelihood of paying anyone back was still years away. His creditors were getting concerned.

Crassus, as always eager to put ambitious men in his debt, came to the rescue, extending Caesar a massive, interest-free loan that was large enough to temporarily satisfy his creditors[67]. The important thing now was to get to Spain. Once there, his future would be in his own hands – to triumph or fail on his own merits. He left before his posting was officially announced, a rare breach of protocol which showed just how important he considered this. The future was at stake. There would be no more delays or interruptions.

---

[66] To escape the anger of the mob on one hand and the anger of the patricians on the other, many of the jurors made the clever decision to make their verdicts completely illegible. They were saved from lynching by their messy handwriting.

[67] According to Plutarch it was roughly 59,000 pounds of gold.

Chapter 10

THE GHOST OF ALEXANDER

"For what is the life of a man, if it is not interwoven with the life of former generations by a sense of history?"

- Cicero

The Caesar who crossed the Alps was a cypher. He was certainly confident, but had never commanded an army, and frankly was widely considered to be a bit of a pretty boy. Stories of his foppish behavior were well known. He had once commissioned a villa in the countryside and then had it immediately torn down again for not living up to his uncompromising standards. His sense of style and charm were undeniable – he could deliver a speech and dress in the latest fashions – but the battlefield was a much different thing[68].

He departed for Spain carrying mosaic flooring to furnish his tent, seemingly the very picture of an effete aristocrat, and yet, once there he ate in the saddle, seemed impervious to cold or damp, and shared everything with his men. He was an impossibly remote figure with the common touch. Such were the contradictions of Caesar. His enemies could comfort themselves in the knowledge that he was a reckless spender, and once the money ran out, the popularity would too. Caesar, in other words, was an easy man to dismiss[69].

One of the only people who had seen beneath the facade was Cicero. Perhaps because he was an outsider himself, he recognized

---

[68] The more perceptive noticed that his frivolity living was more appearance than reality. For all the drinking around him, he rarely indulged himself. As Cato would later write, "*he was the only sober man who tried to overthrow the Republic*".

[69] Insiders usually miss revolutionaries *because* they are insiders. History is full of politically connected experts who misjudged the wolves they let in the door. Sieyes thought he could control Napoleon, von Papen wanted to use Hitler, etc.

something frightening in Caesar. "I fear him", he wrote, "as one fears the smiling aspect of the sea".

Spain would begin to show that those fears were well grounded, even if not everyone was paying attention. There were hidden depths to Caesar. To everyone's surprise, "the dandy with loose fitting clothes" – as Sulla once described him – turned out to be a natural general.

The Iberian Peninsula was a lawless place when Caesar arrived. It had been wracked by several wars, the most recent one being concluded by Pompey a decade before, and the destruction was still visible[70]. Brigandage had become almost a way of life, and in such a climate prosperity, let along stability, was impossible.

Bringing order to this chaos was exactly the sort of task – both administrative and military – that Caesar had hoped for. His first action was to double the size of his garrisons by raising troops from friendly local tribes. He then went on the offensive, campaigning relentlessly against hostile tribes, and trying his best to antagonize peaceful ones. All the hallmarks of his later career were on display; the terrifying speed, the adaptability, and the ruthless exploitation of victory. He avoided ambushes by not taking obvious routes, and constantly threw his enemies off balance by doing the unexpected. In one particularly memorable outing he loaded his men onto oared warships – something that the natives had never seen – and secured the immediate surrender of an unnerved tribe.

He was as generous in peace as he was formidable in war. Like Pompey, he was interested in transforming defeated rivals into productive, tax-paying members of the community. After pacifying the entire province, he reorganized its civil administration, acted as judge in local disputes, and suppressed some of the more cruel practices, which included human sacrifice.

Of course, the main advantage – some would say the whole point – of a provincial posting was to get rich, and Caesar approached this task with his customary zeal. Protection money was collected, plunder

---

[70] Cicero memorably described Pompey's progress through Spain as a "welter of carnage".

was seized, and he developed a reputation for sacking cities after they had surrendered[71].

The province was too impoverished for spectacular gains, but the year was rewarding enough to at least put a dent into his debts, and justify further loans. There were several reasons to be pleased with his first performance as a military governor. Chief among them was the fact that his troops had hailed him as Imperator, a formal acclamation that entitled him to request a triumph when he got back to Rome and would virtually guarantee his election as consul. A triumph was – despite Pompey's celebration of three – an exceptionally rare occurrence. It was the highest honor an aristocrat could earn, and was awarded to only a tiny fraction of generals. These glittering celebrations turned their heroes into larger-than-life figures, and amplified already great reputations. Caesar's name would be on everyone's lips.

The only potential issue was one of protocol. Arranging a suitably grand triumph would take months, but the elections were just a few weeks away. Caesar had to get to the Forum and formally announce his candidacy for the consulship before he could plan his triumph.

But this was more difficult than it seemed. As a commander under arms, Caesar was strictly forbidden from entering Rome. If he crossed the pomerium – the sacred boundary supposedly marked out by Romulus himself – before his term officially expired, his military command would automatically be negated, along with his right to a triumph.

Caesar's solution was to propose that a surrogate should be allowed to announce his candidacy while he prepared the triumphal procession. A letter to this effect was sent to the Senate, requesting a formal exemption from the election law.

The letter was met with widespread disapproval. Caesar's military success was unnerving – no one wanted another Pompey on their hands – and this would be a perfect time to cut him down to size.

---

[71] At least according to his enemies. In many ways this was politics as usual. Caesar himself had prosecuted governors for corruption, but had no trouble collecting bribes.

They had had enough of making exceptions for men who didn't think that the rules applied to them. Cato, as usual, took the lead. When asked his opinion, he started to talk and continued to do so until the sun set, effectively filibustering Caesar's proposal.

For Cato, it was a moment to relish. He loathed Caesar personally, and the fact that his half-sister Servillia was carrying on an affair with the man only made the victory sweeter. By denying the proposal, he had offered Caesar a drink from a poisoned chalice; abandon his triumph forever for the uncertainties of an election, or postpone his political career for at least a year.

Cato most likely was also trying to clear the way for a candidate of his own. His son-in-law, Bibulus, was planning to run for consul, and his chances would be much improved if Caesar was no longer in his way. Unfortunately for Cato, however, he had severely misjudged his man. Popularity was never an allure for Caesar the way it was for Pompey, especially if it came at the expense of power[72].

Caesar didn't even hesitate. Resigning his commission, he immediately crossed the pomerium and entered Rome. The loss of the triumph hurt, but there were greater possibilities ahead and time was short. The elections were just a few weeks away, and he had to gather endorsements, canvass likely voters, and organize his campaign.

Like everything else in Rome, politics was blended with war. It's rare for someone to be truly gifted in both fields; the battlefield calls for a different skill set than that required in the Senate hall. Men like Pompey who excelled in one and are miserable in the other, are the rule, not the exception. Caesar, however, seemed to glide between the two with an uncanny touch; his instincts rarely misled him.

This was particularly useful in Rome, where martial values were woven throughout society. The Romans were – so they believed – descended from the god of war; even the way they voted recalled a warlike past. On election day, the citizens would gather on the field of Mars, the great training ground for the army. There, temporary

---

[72] Cato had forced the same choice on Pompey when the latter applied for his third triumph. Naturally, Pompey chose the triumph.

wooden voting booths called oviles were set up[73]. A red flag would be hoisted up on the nearby Janiculum Hill signaling that all was clear, and the outgoing consul would say a prayer and formally begin the process.

The actual voting was an orderly practice. All adult male citizens were divided into "classes" based on how much property they had owned during the last census. These were further subdivided into "centuries" – the name itself suggests the military origin – and further organized by age[74]. Each century chose two names from the list of candidates, and cast their ballots, which were then tallied and the winners announced. Crucially, the first class voted before anyone else, and its results were made public. Since subsequent classes almost always followed the lead of the first, bribery was particularly powerful. As with any group, there were men of recognized influence who could sway their colleagues. The trick of bribery was to find those willing to exchange their leverage for cash – and to offer more than your opponent did[75].

All this was tremendously expensive, so Caesar proposed a joint campaign with a wealthy senator named Lucius Lucceius. Caesar would provide the popularity and the information on who should be bribed, and Lucceius would provide the money. In addition, Caesar, a prolific letter writer, went on a charm offensive. Suetonius tells us that he could dictate seven letters at a time if they were casual, or two if the topic was important, and he canvassed most of the important men of the Senate[76].

Wooing senators was always a bit of a long shot. He was unlikely to find much support there since Cato and his faction were heavily

---

[73] The *oviles* were fondly referred to as "sheep pens".

[74] There were more than 900,000 eligible voters in Caesar's day. Since the entire process had to be completed by sunset, the vast majority of them could not have participated. How many actually did, of course, is impossible to know, but the consensus opinion seems to have been somewhere between 30,000 and 70,000.

[75] This didn't necessarily have to be upfront. The year before, Pompey had simply told everyone to collect their reward the next day. The sight of them all gathered in his gardens scandalized the city.

[76] His use of letters was considered novel. He may even have used one to divorce his wife Pompeia.

backing Cato's son-in-law, Bibulus. In the end, he didn't need the Senate. When the results were tallied, Caesar easily had the most votes, Bibulus came in second, and poor Lucceius a distant third. The sacrifice of Caesar's triumph had been worth it. He had his consulship. Now it was just a question of what he would do.

If Cato had anything to do with it, the answer would be, nothing. Before a term officially began, it was customary for the Senate to assign the consuls a governorship of a province that they would administer after their consulship ended, and Cato engineered a humiliating assignment for Caesar. Using the recent disturbances of Spartacus as an excuse, the Senate voted to task Caesar and Bibulus with clearing bandits from the woods and paths of Italy when their terms expired. This was announced before the pair even took office, and was a potentially devastating blow.

There were obvious political problems with this, but also financial ones – wandering around the woods of Italy would hardly pay off the debts. Cato's stubbornness had turned him into a one-man wrecking ball. Once he set his mind to something and dug in his heels, there was no way to dislodge him. He couldn't be bribed or reasoned into a different opinion, and his personal bravery made it nearly impossible to intimidate him. Worse yet, he was a master at using parliamentary procedures to stop decisions from being made. The year ahead promised to be a frustrating one.

Caesar wasn't the only one finding out how dangerous Cato's principled stands were. The past several years had been maddening for Pompey and Crassus as well. Cato's anti-corruption stances got in the way of several of Crassus' schemes, and Pompey's proposition for land to settle his veterans had gone nowhere, despite a decade of trying. Cato seemed to take a perverse delight in opposing whatever Pompey proposed. The general's arrangements in the East, for example, were universally regarded as excellent, but Cato stubbornly refused to allow them to be ratified. No matter how many consuls or tribunes Pompey bought, the results were always the same: Pompey the Great couldn't get anything done.

From the start then, Caesar's consulship was faced with a central dilemma. If all of Crassus' wealth and Pompey's popularity couldn't move Cato, what chance was there for Caesar?

Chapter 11

THE THREE-HEADED BEAST

"Nothing could be done in the Republic, which displeased any one of the three."

- Suetonius

The Roman Republic was now at a dangerous crossroads. Its three most powerful men were politically frustrated, and its government seemed defined by corruption and obstruction. If Rome's greatest general and its wealthiest, most connected citizen couldn't get anything done, what hope was there for anyone else?

Caesar had come to the same conclusion, and – as usual – he had an elegant solution. At some point before he officially took office as consul, he paid a visit to both his patron Crassus, and to Pompey. To each he had pointed out a basic truth. None of them could get what they wanted by themselves. Pompey and Crassus lacked an effective surrogate to push through their legislation, and Caesar's consulship would go nowhere without allies. Furthermore, any combination of two of them could be blocked by the third. The only way forward was together.

Caesar had good reason to be insistent. Cato was more than capable of sabotaging everything – he had proved as much this year – and Caesar couldn't afford to be patient. He had sacrificed a triumph for the chance to be consul, and intended to use it to launch a glorious military career like Pompey. That future, however, was only possible if he could somehow get around Cato's vindictive assignment of clearing bandits from the woods of Italy.

The one who needed most convincing was Pompey. He was clearly the greatest of the three, and had never been one to share the spotlight, particularly with Crassus. But, like each of the others, he was desperate, and the possibilities were too tempting. The pairing of Pompey's popularity, Crassus' wealth, and Caesar's political skills would be irresistible. Most delicious of all, Cato and the others would never see it coming. Who would ever believe, after a decade of evidence to the contrary, that Pompey and Crassus would be capable of working together?

The only way they would be able to, of course, was through the intermediary of Caesar. He was both the driving force behind this Triumvirate and the glue holding it together. It was sealed with a pair of weddings. Caesar married Calpurnia, the daughter of one of Crassus' close friends, while Pompey married Caesar's daughter, Julia. The fact that both brides were seventeen, and that Julia happened to already be engaged, was conveniently ignored[77].

For the moment, all three men kept their alliance secret. Caesar seems to have viewed these arrangements as a kind of insurance policy if more traditional methods failed, and he was constantly on the lookout to make their collaboration even stronger.

The only other uncommitted figure of stature in the Republic was Cicero, and a few weeks before Caesar took office he sent a surrogate to court him. There were good reasons to think that Cicero might join the alliance. Although he was by nature a conservative who admired much of what Cato stood for, he fully realized the damage that men like Cato were doing to the Republic.

Caesar offered leadership, and the chance to get things done. The Republic was failing. This was not Caesar's fault, he had simply recognized that fact and exploited it. If the Senate could no longer address the problem, then Caesar would. Perhaps he and the undeniably patriotic Cicero could repair some of the damage and save the Republic.

It was a tempting offer. Cicero would have protection from those still angry at his execution of Roman citizens, a share in power, and security for the rest of his life. Most compellingly of all, he would

---

[77] At 47, Pompey was three decades older than his new wife. Julia had been engaged to a man named Quintus Servilius Caepio who was either the uncle or brother of Brutus.

once again be in the spotlight. After much agonizing, however, Cicero politely declined. He was too much of a patriot to seriously consider hijacking the Republic.

Standing on principle had its price, as Cicero would soon find out, but for the moment Caesar had no wish to antagonize the great orator. His usual policy was to stay on good terms with his colleagues whenever possible, and if that failed, to at least prevent them from becoming active enemies. Cicero's addition to his cause would have lent it rhetorical support, but that was hardly a necessary ingredient.

More pressing was the need to neutralize his co-consul Bibulus, who openly loathed Caesar. Thanks to the age requirements on Roman government positions, and the limited number of candidates who were qualified to run for them each year, the same men tended to compete against each other for every election. As a result, Bibulus' career had run largely parallel to Caesar's. They served as aediles together in 65, praetors in 62, and now consuls in 59. The two men were linked in the public eye, and that wasn't a kind comparison for Bibulus.

Unsurprisingly, he was a member of Cato's conservatives who viewed Caesar as a dangerous rebel and would do everything in his power to obstruct him[78]. Of course, with Pompey and Crassus behind him, Caesar could force anything through, but riding roughshod over tradition had its risks, and could provoke more antagonism than it was worth. Much better to attempt collegiality, or at least its appearance, and let Bibulus be the villain.

As their term began, therefore, Caesar did his best to signal his desire to work together. His inaugural address in the Senate was to that effect, calling for them to put aside personal dislikes for the good of the Republic. In the interests of transparency, and to show that he was interested in good governance, not politics, he announced that all senatorial debates would be transcribed and posted in the Forum as a matter of public record. He was also careful not to upstage his colleague when they appeared in public together, making sure that when it was Bibulus' turn to hold the fasces – the symbol of their

---

[78] Cato's clique also called themselves *boni* – the "good men".

joint consular authority – he followed a discreet distance behind. In contrast to the vindictive Bibulus, Caesar seemed like the very picture of reasonableness.

His first order of business was to pass a bill providing land for Pompey's veterans. This had been continuously blocked by Cato, who was a master of finding things to object to. Caesar's solution was to produce a law so obviously appropriate that any attempt to stop it would be seen as partisan hackery. He leaned hard into this strategy, announcing before introducing his bill, that he would strike out or change any part of it that the Senate objected to. His only desire, he informed his colleagues, was to work together for the benefit of Rome.

This was not the work of a tyrant. The bill called for a land-purchasing commission to be set up – Caesar specifically excluded himself from serving on it – that would be funded by the treasure brought back from Pompey's conquests at no cost to the state. Property would only be bought at a fair price as determined by the last census, and only from those willing to sell it. Finally, the state gifts of land would be opened up to the urban poor as well[79]. This would both alleviate poverty and – since any recipient couldn't sell their land for twenty years – create stable new taxpaying communities.

The bill was so well written that even Cato couldn't find anything to object to. As Caesar began to ask individual senators their opinion, it must have begun to dawn on Cato's clique that Caesar had laid a careful trap. Anything they said in opposition to the bill would sound petty, and since the debate was being recorded and publicly posted, that fact would become obvious to everyone in the city.

As a result, none of the conservatives had anything to say, and it became clear that the bill would pass. Cato, however, wasn't one to be deterred by a little unpopularity. He claimed that the timing wasn't right and then took the floor where he droned on and on about nothing. Talking things to death was Cato's favorite tactic.

---

[79] The law provided land for any poor father with at least three children. The 20,000 families that were awarded land became clients of Julius Caesar.

After a few hours, Caesar's patience snapped. At his signal Cato was arrested, and, still trying to speak, hauled off to prison. This may have been secretly relieving to the assembled senators who had sat through Cato's filibustering before, but it proved to be a political mistake. Cato was a boor, but he had a sacrosanct right to speak. By violating this, Caesar looked like a tyrant, and lost whatever good will he had built up among the moderate senators. This point was driven home when Caesar tried to resume the meeting. An elderly senator struggled to his feet and began to walk toward the doorway. When Caesar asked him why he was leaving, the man answered that he would rather be in prison with Cato than in the Senate with Caesar.

Realizing that he had lost, Caesar dismissed the session and – not wanting to turn Cato into a martyr – quietly ordered his release. It was a rare political miscalculation. For the rest of his term, he refused to call the senators into session, taking all of his business to the assembly of the people instead[80].

The next day, Caesar appeared in the Forum and summoned his colleague Bibulus to explain publicly why he had not supported the land bill. The consul repeated Cato's objections about timing, but the crowd became incensed and started insisting that the bill be passed. At this point Bibulus completely lost his head and shouted that they wouldn't get the bill even if every single one of them wanted it. As the crowd erupted in a fury, he turned on his heel and stormed out.

Caesar couldn't have asked for a better performance. With the crowd in a frenzy, he produced Crassus and Pompey, asking each of them in turn what they thought of the bill. When Caesar asked Pompey what he would do if their enemies tried to use violence to stop the bill, he roared out that he would meet swords with swords. The ecstatic response from the crowd was deafening.

The public appearance of Crassus and Pompey with Caesar sent shockwaves through the Republic. The thought that these three natural enemies could have allied – and had clearly done so before

---

[80] Both the Senate and the Popular Assembly could pass legislation.

Caesar took office – was terrifying[81]. Even some of Pompey's closest supporters were unnerved. Marcus Varro, the man who had provided him with a 'cheat sheet' of senatorial etiquette for his first consulship, called the alliance a "three-headed beast" that would devour the Republic.

In some ways it already had. The triumvirate had effectively displaced the Senate – although that reality was slow to dawn on most of its members. It was Pompey who drove the point home. On the day of the vote, he filled the Forum with armed veterans to ensure a favorable result. Cato and Bibulus showed up with a group of their supporters to break up the meeting, but Pompey would allow no dissenting voices. Both of them were seized, and Bibulus had his symbols of office smashed. When the enraged consul tried to speak, he had a bucket of faeces dumped on his head.

Although several people were injured, the point was to humiliate, not to kill. Bibulus and Cato were physically thrown out of the Forum, and after an unproductive attempt to sneak back in, even Cato realized it was futile to resist any further. This point was reinforced when Caesar added a clause to the bill requiring senators to swear an oath to support it. Any who neglected to take the oath – or who worked to repeal the law – would be immediately exiled[82].

Now that the triumvirate was out in the open, Caesar moved with brutal efficiency to suppress dissent. Cicero, who had so recently been courted by Caesar, made the mistake of mildly criticizing the triumvirate in a speech. Within the day, one of Caesar's surrogates threatened to prosecute him, and Cicero spent the rest of the year in a self-imposed exile on one of his country estates. His house in Rome – on which he had spent a fortune – was demolished by a mob, and a temple to Liberty was erected on the site.

Bibulus, who had not fully understood the significance of recent events, made one final attempt to stop Caesar and appealed to the Senate to strip his colleague of the consulship. But with Pompey's

---

[81] In addition to the well-known animosity between Pompey and Crassus, Caesar had seduced both of his colleague's wives.

[82] Cato was convinced to swear the oath by Cicero who pointed out that he could do more good inside Rome than exiled from it.

men wandering through the streets, no one was foolish enough to vote for the motion. In any case, too many of the senators either feared the triumvirate or owed money to Crassus to block anything they proposed.

Bibulus was politically neutered and he knew it. He spent the rest of the year barricaded inside his house, composing crude insults about Caesar, which were then forwarded to the Senate for the amusement of what friends remained. More cleverly, he attempted to undermine his fellow consul by announcing each day that the omens were unfavorable, and that no official business could therefore be done[83].

This was generally met with a shrug, since everybody was perfectly aware that it was a stunt. Both Pompey and Caesar were priests, and the former specifically belonged to the college that interpreted omens. They simply ignored Bibulus, and everyone else did as well[84].

Having crushed all opponents, Caesar pushed through everything that the triumvirs wanted; Pompey's eastern settlement was ratified, and Crassus got some tax deals[85]. Most satisfying of all, Caesar awarded himself a five-year governorship of Gaul, leaving the 'woods and paths of Italy' for his diminutive colleague to police[86].

The only thing left to do was set up a friendly successor. Technically, Bibulus' stunt with the omens made all of Caesar's legislation illegal, and there was always the possibility that someone would try to invalidate it. To guard against this, Caesar arranged for his father-in-law to be elected consul, ensuring a friendly government to safeguard his interests.

He now had three legions at his disposal, a vast province to be governed, and the promise of spectacular military glory ahead of him. All he had to do was seize the opportunity.

---

[83] On one occasion a mob formed outside his house and asked him to announce his findings in person. He wisely demurred.

[84] Bibulus was so irrelevant that people began referring to the year as the consulship of Julius and Caesar.

[85] Caesar also – in exchange for a hefty bribe – recognized the rule of Ptolemy XII over Egypt. The new pharaoh was the father of Cleopatra.

[86] Unsurprisingly, Bibulus declined to take up his commission.

Chapter 12

CARPE DIEM

"Roman, remember by your strength to rule Earth's peoples...To pacify, to impose the rule of law, to spare the conquered, battle down the proud."

- Virgil

It was in Gaul that Caesar became Caesar. At forty-two he wasn't old by Roman standards, but there was a faint sense that time had passed him by. Pompey had found glory in his twenties, and Alexander the Great – against whom Julius Caesar constantly measured himself – never reached his thirty-third birthday. None of his contemporaries could have guessed that this middle-aged man would soon prove to be one of the greatest generals of all time.

The fact that he had selected Gaul as a proving ground was itself a telling choice. It was a wild and savage land, beyond the lights of the civilized world. A tiny fraction of it had been claimed by Rome, but even these provinces were little more than some lines on a map, a vague agreement between the Senate and various strongmen who paid lip service to Rome while constantly fighting each other[87]. The shifting alliances and eternal conflict represented a kind of primeval chaos that was deeply upsetting to the orderly Roman mind.

The Republic had always been afraid of what lay beyond the Alps. In the fourth century BC, wild Gauls had swept down from the mountains like a mighty flood, and brutally sacked Rome. Galloping through the streets with the heads of their enemies dangling from the

---

[87] Roman Gaul was divided into two separate provinces. Transalpine Gaul – "Gaul beyond the Alps" – included the coastal strip of land between the Pyrenees and the Alps. The more civilized Cisalpine Gaul, also called *Gallia Togata* – "toga-wearing Gaul" was essentially northern Italy. Caesar was governor of both of them.

necks of their horses, they had slaughtered indiscriminately, setting fire to everything they couldn't steal or kill. The memory of that event still haunted the Romans more than three centuries later, along with the fear that the next wave of attacks would snuff out the light for good[88].

This was all the more horrifying because the Roman mind was obsessed with order. The poet Virgil, writing a generation after Caesar, reminded his countrymen that Rome's obligation was "to impose the rule of law" on a chaotic world. He may very well have been referring to Gaul. The very fear which clawed at Roman hearts was what made Gaul's conquest a worthy challenge. What better way for Caesar to earn his reputation than by piercing the very heart of darkness itself?

As if to heighten the stakes, word of an impending disaster arrived before he even left Rome. In the central plateau of what is today Switzerland, a confederation of tribes called the Helvetii had begun a migration westward into Transalpine Gaul. As a sign of their determination, they burned their own villages, loaded up their possessions into carts, and began moving en masse into the valleys of Transalpine Gaul. All the old nightmares were reawakened. Conservative Roman estimates put their numbers at 300,000; if they decided to turn towards Italy, there would be no stopping them.

One of Caesar's gifts was an ability to both think and act with a speed that left his enemies disoriented and off balance. He left for his province in the early spring of 58, covering the more than five hundred miles between Rome and Geneva in a mere seven days. Realizing that the barbarian numbers were closer to four hundred thousand than three, he raised two additional legions from scratch, sealed the border to his province, and ambushed them when they tried to go north into the non-Roman part of Gaul. After two vicious battles, the Helvetii sued for peace, and were sent back to their burned alpine homes as the newest subjects of Rome.

---

[88] Thanks to the timely honking of some sacred geese during the attack, the buildings of the Capitoline hill were saved by the alerted garrison. The guard dogs who had failed to bark were killed, and as a continuing punishment, each year a dog was publicly crucified, while a goose was brought to watch the ceremony from its perch on a purple cushion.

As word of the victory spread, Gallic requests for help began
to pour in. For more than a decade, Germanic tribesmen had been
crossing the Rhine, pushing the natives back. Under the command
of an ambitious figure named Ariovistus, the Germans had settled in
what is now Flanders, and had seized control of northeastern Gaul.
Somewhat embarrassingly, Ariovistus was officially an ally of Rome,
and had been made so by none other than Caesar himself during his
year as consul.

Now he had a chance to correct this oversight. He had long since
come to the conclusion that the Germans were a menace to Rome's
interests in Gaul, as indeed were the constantly shifting alliances of
the natives. The only solution was to expel the Germans and then
bring all of Gaul – from the Alps to the North Sea – under the Roman
yoke.

As always, Caesar attempted diplomacy first by inviting Ariovistus
to a meeting to discuss their positions. The Germanic warlord rejected
it out of hand, pointedly suggesting that Caesar should mind his own
business[89]. He then mobilized his army, allowing Caesar to claim
that he was acting in self-defense for the security of his province,
and beyond that, of Rome itself. The two armies met on a lightly
wooded field in what is now Bavaria, about ten miles west of the
Rhine. Despite being outnumbered by nearly a hundred thousand
men, Caesar smashed the Germanic horde, killing or capturing nearly
all of them.

He followed up this brilliant victory by letting the Gauls know
that their days of independence were numbered. Marching his legions
a hundred miles north of the Roman border, deep inside the territory
of an officially neutral Gallic tribe, he built winter quarters. While
camped there – without even bothering to inform the Senate – he
raised and equipped two fresh legions at his own expense, doubling
the amount of troops that he had legally been given.

As soon as the weather permitted, he went on the offensive.
Nearly a dozen Gallic tribes had allied against him, but he seemed to

---

[89] He also pointed out that he was merely doing what the Romans themselves
had done all over the Mediterranean.

be everywhere at once, pushing them back. Crisscrossing lands that had never before seen a legionary, Caesar advanced as far as the coast of the North Sea.

The Gallic plan was to overwhelm the invader through sheer force of numbers, but they had never faced an enemy like Caesar. He was relentless, pursuing them through tangled forests and across scorched fields. Like a great knot coming undone, the Gallic alliance began to crumble. Every victory led to further defections as individual tribes came to the conclusion that peace was sweeter than freedom.

Caesar's soldiers were also beginning to realize that he was unlike other Roman generals. It wasn't just his tactical brilliance, although that was certainly appreciated. There was something more, some indefinable charisma that both inspired and demanded loyalty. He had exacting standards, but he never asked something of his men that he was unwilling to do himself. He slept where they slept, ate what they ate, and referred to them as his "fellows". They responded with fanatical devotion.

Not only did his soldiers fight better for Caesar than for other commanders, but they endured far more as well. To keep them sharp, he would abruptly start a long and brutal march – at times in the middle of the night – at breakneck speed. This must have been a horrific experience since Caesar himself was capable of extreme endurance. Those who kept up with him were praised, while those who lagged behind were excoriated. They were Caesar's men, and therefore much was expected of them.

There were greater allowances too. After victorious battles Caesar would divide up the loot equally among them, without taking a greater share for himself. Other generals would strictly control what their troops did in their off time, but Caesar allowed his to do whatever they pleased. When one senator criticized his men for visiting brothels, Caesar dryly responded that they fought just as well while stinking of perfume. The only thing that mattered was how they performed in battle.

His men responded by absorbing Caesar's obsession with honor. There was no worse crime than running from battle, and no greater punishment than Caesar's disappointment. Those who dropped their weapons and ran were worse than dead. They were traitors and cowards, unworthy to be Caesar's men.

Their courage at times verged on madness. On one occasion, several centurions were cut off from the army by a group of Gauls. As Caesar watched, one of his men crashed into the barbarian line, single-handedly cutting his way through and rescuing the trapped men. In the heavy fighting that followed, the soldier was nearly killed, but managed to claw his way back to the Roman line. As Caesar was praising him for his bravery, the man fell sobbing at his feet, begging his general to forgive him for returning without his shield.

It was rare for Caesar to be on the defensive. More often than not it was his men who were administering stinging defeats. Caesar's spies – wine merchants who had penetrated further into Gaul than any soldier – kept him one step ahead of his enemies, and the relentlessness of his advance wore them down[90]. The waterways of Gaul became so choked with corpses that one writer claimed that the legionnaires could cross rivers without getting their feet wet. Meanwhile, in Italy, the glutted slave markets sold Gallic prisoners for a single amphora of wine. Such a horrific human cost was too much to bear, and after three seasons of campaigning, the tribes that had opposed him surrendered unconditionally. Caesar could now write to the Senate that all of Gaul had been subdued.

Caesar's governorship extended to lands on both sides of the Alps, and his campaigning in what is now France had meant a long absence from the territory in Northern Italy. Now that Gaul had been conquered, he could attend to these lands as well. He re-crossed the Alps and busied himself with the routine tasks of governing. Legal disagreements were settled, taxes were levied, and administrative duties were discharged. Most importantly of all, his soldiers were given a much-needed rest, and their numbers were brought back up to strength.

---

[90] The wine merchants were so effective at intelligence gathering that the Germanic tribes east of the Rhine banned the sale of wine in their territory on the grounds that it made men soft.

As triumphant as all this undoubtedly was, his literary output was even more impressive. While constantly campaigning, he had somehow found time to send regular dispatches home, keeping the Roman people advised of his every move. It was common for generals to keep records for later memoirs, but this was the first time that a Roman general was reporting directly from the front lines.

Despite the speed with which they were composed, these reports were more than simple, unpolished notes. Caesar was a gifted writer, and his Commentaries – the first example of Latin historical prose in history – were best-sellers from the start.

Caesar's genius was partially in his ability to control a narrative. The conquest of Gaul was framed as a fundamentally defensive campaign, a continuous struggle against the menace of hostile tribes. All the illegal steps that he had taken were carefully explained as necessary and proper responses to Gaulish aggression. Always, his primary motivation was to extend peace, stability, and Roman civilization.

Despite this, Caesar made no attempt to disguise the more brutal consequences of defying Rome. When one tribe offered to surrender but then launched a surprise attack during the negotiations, Caesar wiped them out, selling all fifty-three-thousand survivors as slaves in a single sale[91]. Another tribe, the Nervii, reported that of sixty thousand warriors, only five hundred remained after fighting the Romans.

The two sides were clearly defined, but Caesar's depiction of Gaul was never one of cartoonish opposites. He generally refrained from dehumanizing his opponents, focusing instead on their inherent nobility. The Gallic desire to escape the Roman yoke may have been misguided, but it was presented as perfectly understandable. At times he referred to them as "brothers", and pointed out how much they had in common with the Romans. Both struggled with corruption, had to pay taxes, and had similar social structures with slaves at the

---

[91] This is not just a literary conceit. Archeological evidence shows that their settlements in what is now Belgium remained unoccupied for the next two centuries.

bottom and an aristocratic class at the top. They were, in short, fit to be part of the Roman body.

This subtle presentation was reported with a simple style that lacked the rhetorical flourishes so popular at the time. Cicero perceptively noticed the effect that his reports had on the poorer classes who seemed most enthusiastic about Caesar. As he knew first hand, eloquence and style combined to make very effective propaganda. When news reached Rome that Caesar had conquered Gaul, the Senate, spurred on by the people and Cicero himself, voted to observe an unprecedented fifteen days of sacrifices and public holiday.

But despite the adulation, all was not well in Rome. Caesar's rise had attracted much attention, and as always, forces were gathering to pull down a too-ambitious man. Already there were calls to undo all of Caesar's legislation and try him for war crimes[92]. Even worse, the triumvirate itself was on the verge of collapse.

---

[92] Caesar's enemies in Rome used his own words against him. His term of office hadn't expired, which should have protected him from litigation. But since he had claimed that the war was won, there was no need for him to remain in Gaul and he could therefore be brought home and tried.

Chapter 13

LUCA

"This is tyranny's disease, to trust no friends"

- Aeschylus

The agreement between Pompey, Caesar, and Crassus had always been built on an unstable foundation. The three were natural enemies – all were ambitious men – and their alliance would last only as long as each believed that it was serving their ends. The moment any one of them saw an advantage elsewhere, the entire construct would collapse.

Crassus and Pompey's animosities were always bubbling just beneath the surface, and without Caesar's influence, they had started to drift apart. This was a serious problem because even at the peak of their cooperation, they were limited in how much they could control. Cato and his allies still had a significant amount of power, and there were other ambitious men operating outside – and against – the interests of the triumvirate. Chief among these was Publius Clodius Pulcher.

The Bona Dea scandal had only encouraged his wild behavior, which was not entirely surprising. The only thing more impressive than the Claudian's blue-blood was their arrogance which – even for the nobility – was legendary[93].

Clodius was a born demagogue, who masked considerable political savvy underneath an obnoxious facade. He knew exactly what kinds of opportunities the triumvirate opened up, and didn't hesitate to use violence to accomplish his goals.

---

[93] When a crowded street obstructed the progress of one of Clodius' ancestors, she had loudly suggested that Rome's poor should be drowned to alleviate the congestion.

His newest scheme was to position himself as the great champion of the people by running for the office of tribune of the plebs. Since this office was only open to a commoner, he gave up his patrician status and got himself adopted into a plebeian family[94].

Caesar had been more than happy to let this go forward, and as consul had formally granted Clodius permission to be adopted. A little electoral chaos wasn't necessarily a bad thing, and Clodius thanked him by hiring a gang of thugs and going after Caesar's enemies.

Though he preferred brute force, Clodius was subtle enough to neutralize his opponents in other ways as well. When the prosperous island of Cyprus was annexed by the Republic, Clodius cleverly arranged for Cato to be sent to oversee the details of the transfer. This had the advantage of removing the stubborn senator from the senate and of depriving the conservatives of their leadership.

He had done a great service to Caesar, but Clodius was too much of a wild card to be an effective tool. He served no one's interest but his own, and the taste of power was far too intoxicating to give up. He was popular, ambitious, and thanks to his gangs had a near total control of the streets. Why play second fiddle to the triumvirate?

The power that the three triumvirs wielded was deeply resented, and this was adroitly used by Clodius to increase his own popularity. Anything that made one of them look foolish – or better yet powerless – would be applauded, and the unsuspecting Pompey made a perfect target.

On one of his eastern campaigns, Pompey had captured a prince of Armenia and was now keeping him confined in his mansion as a potential bargaining chip. Clodius arranged for some of his men to break into Pompey's house and smuggle the prince out, which made Pompey look incompetent and weak. When Pompey responded by having one of the consuls formally protest, Clodius' gang beat the poor man within an inch of his life.

---

[94] The plebeians were commoners and their tribune was to serve their interests. Needless to say, the hypocrisy of the blue-blooded Clodius posing as the champion of the people was breathtaking.

Pompey seemed to be in shock, so Clodius gleefully attacked the triumvir directly. He used his influence among the common people to whip up resentment against Pompey, and the great man began to be booed in public[95]. Clodius then had one of his slaves drop a dagger in public, and "confess" that he had been sent to assassinate Pompey. Seriously unnerved, Pompey barricaded himself inside his house.

Clodius was thrilled. He had the triumvirate on the run. He targeted the absent Caesar, suggesting that his entire consulship had been illegal, and that all his legislation should therefore be overturned[96]. In a cheeky bit of gamesmanship, Clodius even called Caesar's erstwhile colleague, Bibulus, as a witness for the prosecution.

The damage to the power of the triumvirate was felt immediately. In that year's elections Pompey – from the safety of his mansion – officially endorsed several candidates. The support of one of the triumvirs should have been enough to guarantee victory by itself, but Pompey was worried enough to also sponsor lavish games to woo the voters. He was right to be concerned. In a stunning rejection of the triumvirate most of Pompey's candidates lost anyway.

The humiliation finally convinced Pompey to fight fire with fire. When Clodius' year as tribune ended, Pompey supported an ex-gladiator named Titus Milo to take his place. Milo was a brawler who had his own gang of thugs, and knew exactly what was expected of him. He took the innovative step of using gladiators and ex-soldiers to stiffen the ranks of his street toughs. Clodius was not one to back down, or see his profitable power base threatened, and soon the capital was plunged into a never-ending turf war. The violence interrupted the flow of grain into the city, and got so bad that all government activity virtually stopped.

The triumvirate had carved up the city, but now they seemed incapable of running it. The underlying reason was that the relationship between the triumvirs had completely broken down.

---

[95] At the performance of a play that Pompey was watching, one of the actors drew great applause when he emphasized the line "You are *great* through our misery".

[96] The irony of course, is that Caesar oversaw his adoption as a plebeian. If *all* of Caesar's acts were illegal, then so were Clodius'.

Contemporaries could hardly fail to notice that Crassus had taken no part in any of the recent events, simply watching as his colleagues were targeted without lifting a finger in their defense.

He had always been at odds with Pompey, but in the past he had been at least able to give the illusion that the two of them were working together. Now, however, there were rumors that he was tacitly backing Clodius – how else to explain the man's continued survival – and perhaps even actively plotting to murder Pompey.

If Crassus was aware of these rumors, he certainly did nothing to dispel them. A note of jealousy had begun to creep in towards Caesar as well. The conspicuous hole in Crassus' resume was a military reputation, and watching a former client outpace him, was alarming.

For his part, Pompey found it easy to believe the worst rumors about Crassus, and in the paranoid atmosphere he began to turn on Caesar as well. Popularity was always a touchy subject for Pompey, and the fact that Caesar had been awarded fifteen days of celebration for a victory over the Gauls when he had only received ten for his magnificent eastern campaign, irked him. He began to confide in friends that he was thinking about divorcing Caesar's daughter, and hinted to Cicero that he now regretted joining the triumvirate. When a conservative tribune proposed the immediate recall of Caesar and his replacement with a consul, Pompey gave only a half-hearted protest, and Crassus didn't say anything at all[97].

The moment Caesar got wind of these events, he realized the danger he was in. Since he obviously couldn't trust Pompey or Crassus to guard his interests, the triumvirate was effectively dead. The only solution was to convince the other two that they could still profit most from working together. This task was too sensitive to be left to intermediaries, it had to be done in person.

Since Caesar was barred from entering Rome while commanding legions, his colleagues travelled north to meet him in his winter quarters at the Tuscan city of Luca. The triumvirs met in mid-April of 56, and over the course of several discussions, Caesar, who had

---

[97] The consul who proposed to take his place was Lucius Domitius Ahenobarbus, a direct ancestor of the emperor Nero.

probably been communicating with both of them for several weeks, managed to convince them to work together again.

His pitch was elegantly simple. All of their frustrations stemmed from the fact that although each of them had immense influence, neither Pompey nor Crassus had any constitutional power. They had to work indirectly through subordinates – and many times incapable ones – to get anything done. Fortunately, Caesar had a solution. Pompey and Crassus would be elected consul for the following year, and they would renew Caesar's Gallic command for another five years. In addition, both Pompey and Crassus would also be granted military commands for the same amount of time, to ensure that they weren't overshadowed by Caesar. Pompey would be governor of Spain and Crassus would have proconsular authority in Syria.

Although they met in private, the conference at Luca was hardly a secret, and when word got out that the triumvirs were meeting, most Romans who had political aspirations wanted to be there too. More than two hundred senators showed up, eager to pledge their support in exchange for choice appointments or other rewards[98].

The triumvir's plans- including the campaigns of Pompey and Crassus – were funded by the spoils Caesar had gotten from Gaul. There was no longer any need to dodge creditors; rivers of gold were sent to Rome to buy votes, reward supporters, and start vast public building projects to keep Caesar's name on everyone's lips.

The results of the negotiations – and Caesar's largess – were immediately apparent. Support for a bill curbing Caesar's power collapsed, and when one of Cato's minions tried to bring it directly to the people they rejected it as well. What gold couldn't buy, violence ensured. Only one candidate dared to run against the triumvirs, and Pompey simply had his thugs prevent the man from entering the forum. When Cato, newly returned from Cyprus, tried to force his way in anyway, he was wounded in the arm and his slave was killed.

---

[98] One senator who did not make the trip was Cicero. The arrangements at Luca were particularly bitter for him, and he had no illusions about what it meant for the Republic or for his own political hopes.

Pompey's men were everywhere, and even the still dangerous Clodius found it wise to select different targets. Rival candidates were beaten up or intimidated into withdrawing, and the Popular Assemblies were dissolved if they leaned in the wrong direction.

There were still some scenes of defiance. Cato, of course, refused to be intimidated and successfully ran for praetor, but Pompey didn't allow him to take office despite the fact that he had obviously received the most votes. The conservatives in the Senate tried to resist as much as they could – one debate grew so heated that Crassus punched a colleague in the face – but the ending was never in doubt. Political courage has always been a rare thing, and most senators simply fell in line. Cicero spoke for many when he wrote, "let me take care that those who have the power shall love me".

The great orator had come to this realization painfully. He had been recalled by Pompey the previous year, in what had seemed at the time like a glorious triumph. Fittingly for a man once hailed as the father of his country, the Senate had voted 416 – 1 to bring him home, and the people had roared their approval[99]. So many cheering fans showed up as he reached Rome that it had taken the entire day for him to get to his lodgings. Wherever he went, he was greeted with loud applause and calls to speak. It was, as he immodestly observed, more like an ascension than a simple homecoming.

It had been doubly crushing, therefore, to discover that he was merely a pawn in the plan to further neutralize Clodius. His role, as Pompey made clear, was to push the triumvir's agenda, not share in their power or decision-making. The fact that he had only himself to blame for this since he had refused Caesar's original offer to join the triumvirate, was no comfort at all. "I must submit to be a servant," he confided bitterly, "I who refused to be one of the masters".

Now he was no more than the mouthpiece of the regime. The legislation that he proposed made the triumvirs virtual dictators. The commands in Syria, Gaul, and Spain were confirmed and all three received the power to levy troops and declare war without the pretense of asking the Senate or the people of Rome.

---

[99] The one 'nay' vote was Clodius.

Thoughtful Romans like Cicero were appalled. Officially, of course, they had to welcome the new arrangements. Cicero gave an eloquent speech in the Senate arguing against any diminution of the triumvir's powers. In private, however, he lamented that the Republic had been mortally wounded at Luca. Among Pompey's notebooks, he grimly confided to a friend, were lists of past and future officials. The Roman government was now a Republic only in name. Freedom was no longer within reach. "Peace" he wrote, "is the best we can hope for now."

Chapter 14

DISTANT LANDS

"The winds and the waves are always on the side of the ablest navigators"

- Gibbon

Peace was one thing that Gaul didn't have. In the winter of 56, while Caesar had been putting out political fires, two Germanic tribes – four hundred and thirty thousand strong according to Caesar – had crossed the Rhine and entered what is now Belgium. These tribes were nothing like those that the Romans had faced. They prized courage and toughness, qualities they gained by eliminating any practice that encouraged weakness. They bathed in icy rivers, and – so Gaulish merchants breathlessly reported – hunted the monsters that lurked in the dark forests beyond the Rhine.

The rumors of Germanic prowess spread a panic through Caesar's camp. Many of his fresh recruits had been drawn by his reputation and the rewards to be gained by serving one of the triumvirs, not by being on the receiving end of a barbarian invasion. Capture by one of these brutes meant enslavement or worse, drowned in a bog or hung from a tree along with those the Germans considered traitors or cowards.

Instead of trying to calm his men, Caesar responded by confronting the rumors directly. He confirmed that the Germans were indeed formidable, and even exaggerated their martial skill. Then he announced that he would be taking only one legion – the 10th – to fight them since the rest of the army was clearly scared. The 10th was his favorite legion, composed of troops that he had recruited in Spain, and they had taken part in every one of his major military engagements. The 10th would have all the glory to themselves.

The shaming worked. There was an immediate uproar with the rank and file shouting abuse at their officers who had let Caesar believe they were frightened. The 10th legion sent deputies to Caesar's tent with gratitude and promises that they would be worthy, and the rest of the army sent men to beg him to let them come.

Using his trademark speed, Caesar force marched his now fired-up troops north and met the Germans near what is today Xanten in northwestern Germany. The tribes were taken by surprise and after a short skirmish, they sent their leaders to negotiate. Hardly believing his luck, Caesar imprisoned the chiefs and ordered an immediate attack on the now rudderless horde. It was less of a battle than a massacre with the Roman forces driving the Germans back to the Rhine, butchering everyone, including women and children, who hadn't drowned.

A single victory, however, wasn't enough. The Germans on the far side of the Rhine had clearly not yet learned to fear Roman arms. Unless they were taught otherwise, they would continue to cross with impunity, destabilizing Gaul and providing an eternal source of aid for would-be Gallic rebels.

Caesar's instincts, in war as in politics, were always to overawe his enemies and keep them off balance through boldness and quick action. A grand gesture, coming out of nowhere, could dazzle into submission. It was time to subject the Germans with a display of Roman power. The Rhine river was one of the great barriers of Europe, with treacherous currents and unpredictable shallows. Any large group that tried to navigate it would inevitably be scattered, and fall easy prey if they were observed by a force on the other bank.

Caesar had conquered the invaders, now he proposed to conquer the river by building a bridge[100]. Choosing a particularly turbulent spot, in full view of the watching Germans, he began work. Legionnaires were repurposed as workmen, hacking down trees and hauling them to the bank. The engineering feat alone drove the point home. In ten days the bridge – thirty feet wide and thirteen hundred feet long with protecting forts at each end- was completed.

---

[100] He claimed that a ferry was "beneath his dignity".

Caesar could now cross at will, in perfect order and safety, which he immediately did. There was no one waiting on the other end. The Germans had vanished into their forests before the bridge was even half-finished. Caesar made no attempt to follow them. Instead he spent eighteen days burning as many villages and crops as he could find. Then, having made his point, he recrossed the magnificent bridge, tearing it down behind him.

The destruction only underscored his message. This feat of engineering that the Germanic tribes were incapable of, was not even worth preserving. He had, as he wrote in his Commentaries, given the Germans a taste of fear, and driven home the point that he could – and would – cross the Rhine whenever he wanted to. From that moment on, they would invade Gaul at their own peril.

Though it was now late in the summer, Caesar had an even more spectacular exploit planned. He had taught all of Gaul to fear Roman arms, but now it was time to extend that lesson beyond the borders of the known world.

Caesar was restless with limits. The mere presence of an obstacle like the Rhine was an invitation to overcome it. To the north, like a siren, lay the great ocean, an impenetrable river that encircled the globe. Some of the more intrepid merchants reported that there was a fog-shrouded island there, dripping in gold, pearls, and precious metals. Others denied that it existed at all, pointing out no one had actually explored this mysterious island. But Caesar was confident that Britain was out there, and the common knowledge that barbarians got more ferocious the further north one went, made it irresistible[101]. In July of 55 he gathered two legions near modern-day Calais, and loaded them on to thirty-eight hastily gathered transports.

Caesar's justification of the raid – and it was far too late in the season to be anything but that – was the rather unconvincing claim that it was merely to punish the islanders for providing aid to some Gallic rebels. The first sight of Britain seemed ominous to his soldiers. Cicero's brother Quintus, serving as one of Caesar's legates, wrote that "it lurked in the fog and mist like another planet". One glimpse of

---

[101] One of the more ghastly rumors was that the northern savages drank milk.

the natives confirmed this feeling. They had blue-painted skin, wildly spiked hair, and rode chariots like some kind of Homeric nightmare.

It was so unnerving that when it came time to disembark, no one moved. Finally, the standard-bearer of Caesar's favorite legion plunged into the pounding surf, holding nothing but the eagle, daring his comrades to let it be captured by the enemy. That broke the spell. The rest of the soldiers sprang forward and, after a short struggle, forced a beachhead.

This rocky start only got worse. Rough seas had forced the eighteen cavalry transports to turn back, depriving Caesar of his most effective force. Even worse, as a child of the gentler Mediterranean, he was inexperienced with the more severe Atlantic tides, and had failed to correctly anchor his ships. A full moon and its accompanying surge saw twelve ships destroyed and many others swamped.

Realizing that their enemy was now marooned and vulnerable, the watching Britons attacked, nearly overwhelming the Romans with their first charge. Only the charisma of Caesar himself saved the situation, as he leapt into the fray where the fighting was most desperate, and managed to rally his troops.

The victory bought Caesar breathing room, and he used it to demand hostages, burn several villages, and repair his ships. There was very little else he could do. The weather had already turned with late summer storms lashing his camp, and most of the natives had decided to simply withdraw and wait till this new invader left.

As soon as his transports were seaworthy, Caesar obliged, recrossing the Channel and writing to the Senate that he had met with his "usual success". This was, of course, highly misleading – the invasion had nearly been a disaster, and had provided nothing at all of lasting value – but it was a magnificent propaganda coup. The news that a Republican army had successfully crossed the ocean caught the Roman imagination and demanded a sequel. The Senate, spurred on by the excitement of the people, voted to hold twenty days of public thanksgiving for Caesar's exploit.

Chapter 15

BRITAIN

"All bad fortune is to be conquered by endurance"

- Virgil

C aesar may have been back in Gaul, but Britain was clearly still on his mind. During the winter he ordered the construction of a massive fleet large enough to carry five legions and two thousand cavalry across the Channel[102]. To compensate for the heavy surf of the last invasion, he had the ships built with shallow drafts to allow them to get closer to the shore and enable the men to get on land more quickly.

The native Britons took one look at the size of the force and retreated, allowing Caesar to land unmolested at what is now Sandwich Bay near the mouth of the Great Stour River. He went on the offensive immediately. Leaving a legion and some cavalry to protect the ships, he marched twelve miles under the cover of darkness into modern-day Kent.

Caesar's speed and aggressiveness had thrown the British off balance, and they melted away before the Roman advance. The first real opposition came near Canterbury, where a loose confederation of tribes had gathered in a citadel. Caesar ordered an immediate assault, and after a short battle, the natives scattered.

Caesar's instinct was to keep up the pressure while his enemies were on the run, but as evening approached, word reached him that a coastal storm had struck his fleet. This was a potentially devastating blow. He was heavily outnumbered in a hostile and unfamiliar

---

[102] This was the largest military crossing of the English Channel until D-Day almost two thousand years later.

country, and now his ability to retreat might have been compromised. He returned immediately to find that the damage was even worse than he had feared. Forty of his transports were completely demolished, and the rest were either swamped or leaking.

The sight of wreckage demoralized his soldiers who were now facing the prospect of surviving a brutal winter in alien territory. Caesar, however, kept his head and immediately took charge of the situation. A boat that was still seaworthy was sent speeding to Gaul with instructions to start building ships as quickly as possible. In the meantime, the legionnaires were tasked with patching hulls and making repairs. In only ten days, the work was done. Enough ships had been fixed to evacuate the legions if necessary, and the advance could resume.

The ten day intermission had given the Britons time to recover from the initial shock of the invasion, and they had organized resistance around a local chief named Cassivellaunus. It didn't take him long to realize that the Britons were no match for the Romans in the field. There were other ways to win a victory, however. It was now late summer, and if he could prevent the Romans from crossing the Thames River, he could simply wait for the deteriorating weather to drive them back to Gaul. There was only one fordable spot within easy reach; all the British had to do was fortify it before the Romans arrived.

Cassivellaunus began to use guerrilla tactics to slow Caesar's advance. He set ambushes and used his superior knowledge of the terrain to launch furious diversionary raids with his war chariots. Although Caesar repelled each of these assaults, the courage of the Britons impressed him. He included in his Commentaries a vivid depiction of a native attack. The sound that the chariots made was unnerving, as was their occupant's dexterity. Even on steep slopes they could control their horses at a full gallop, and could dart from the chariot to their horses and back again, where they would unload a furious barrage of spears. When their missiles were thrown, they dismounted and fought on foot, with their chariots standing by if they were routed. That way, as Caesar pointed out, "they have the mobility of cavalry and the staying power of infantry".

When Caesar reached the Thames near present-day central London, he found Cassivellaunus' army blocking his path. With his characteristic energy he attacked at once, inflicting a crushing defeat on the natives[103]. The victory was a serious blow to Cassivellaunus' authority, and his alliance began to crumble. Six tribes crossed over to Caesar, offering an alliance in exchange for Rome's protection. As a sign of their goodwill, they sent hostages, grain, and guides to lead the Roman army to Cassivellaunus' stronghold.

As Caesar closed in, Cassivellaunus managed to get word to four Kentish tribes who agreed to head for the coast to attack the Roman fleet while the main force was away. The single legion stationed there, however, not only defeated them, but managed to capture one of the chieftains. News of this defeat effectively ended resistance to Caesar, although the beleaguered Cassivellaunus held out for a few more days.

By the early fall, Caesar had arranged various peace treaties, accepted hostages, and extracted promises from the coastal tribes to cease providing aid to Gaul. It was this last stipulation that was the most important. Roman control over the British tribes was ephemeral at best – as Caesar knew well. Despite all the claims of fealty to Rome, there would be no Roman presence in Britain for another century. Caesar, of course would claim to have conquered, but his main goal was the stability of Roman Gaul and that depended on neutralizing outside threats. His British excursion – like his German one – had accomplished this. There was no further evidence of British aid to Gallic rebels after Caesar returned.

---

[103] A second century source claimed that he used an elephant he had brought over from Gaul to force the river, but Caesar himself attributed the victory to the "speed and ferocity" of his soldiers. Britain would have to wait another century for the emperor Claudius to see an elephant.

Chapter 16

VERCINGETORIX

"Human nature is universally imbued with a desire for liberty, and a hatred for servitude"

- Caesar

Caesar had promised Rome that Gaul was pacified, yet it was anything but. Roman control was merely a thin veneer, masking a deep and violent resentment. Even before he had re-crossed the Channel, there were signs of trouble. The harvest had failed and it didn't take long for the entire province to be seething with revolt. All that winter and the following summer Caesar was forced to criss-cross Gaul, stamping out isolated revolts wherever they flared up[104]. But he couldn't be everywhere at once.

Garrisons he left behind were constantly pressured and occasionally ambushed. In one particularly violent episode an entire camp of seven thousand legionnaires was wiped out. The constant harassment began to fray Roman nerves.

The revolts were still isolated events, without a hint of coordination. To keep it this way, Caesar encouraged infighting among the Gauls by turning over the land of rebellious tribes to their neighbors to do with as they pleased. By the fall of 53, this strategy of divide and conquer seemed to have worked. The exhausted Caesar felt secure enough to retire to his winter quarters in Ravenna, leaving his army concentrated in northern Gaul.

That winter was more bitter than most, and Caesar spent his time administering the long-neglected part of his province south of the Alps. He also found time to write and publish two books of his

---

[104] He even found time to recross the Rhine to prevent the Germans from taking advantage of the unrest.

Commentaries, announcing once again that Gaul was pacified – a preliminary step in his triumphal return to Rome. In the midst of these preparations he heard of the fate of his fellow triumvir, Crassus.

Caesar's exploits in Gaul had left Crassus feeling overshadowed. It was one thing to have Pompey – Rome's most famous general – outshine him, but quite another for his one-time client to do the same. Crassus was in danger of becoming an afterthought, and needed to burnish his resumé. A little military glory would go a long way toward evening the scales.

He chose Syria as a theater for typical reasons. The eastern boundary of his territory was the Euphrates, across which lay lands of untold wealth[105]. The only obstacle to these riches was the Parthian empire which – conveniently enough – bordered Syria. All he needed to do was provoke a war with them, mop up whatever resistance they could offer, and return home a conquering hero.

There were plenty of people uneasy with this plan. Crassus was nearly sixty and almost deaf, quite old for a field commander, especially since he hadn't seen action for sixteen years. His only real military experience as a general had come fighting an army of slaves, and Rome was currently on fine terms with the Parthians.

But Crassus wasn't one to be easily discouraged once he had put his mind to something. His son, Publius Crassus, fresh from service with Caesar would accompany him and share the burdens of command. Publius had distinguished himself in Gaul and joined his father with a thousand exotic natives in tow. It was widely assumed that he would more than make up for any deficiencies of the elder Crassus.

In the summer of 54 Crassus' armies crossed the Euphrates, seized a couple of border towns, and provoked the Parthians into declaring war. In typical fashion, however, Crassus decided not to invade immediately, but to concentrate on systematically ransacking his own province first.

---

[105] Some of the more credulous tales featured cities with walls made of pearl, and entire mountains of pure gold.

A year was spent carefully looting and levying taxes. Nothing was spared. Villas were despoiled, temples were stripped, and every spare copper was squeezed from the populace[106]. These funds were then used to recruit and arm seven legions, a force nearly equal to Caesar's in Gaul.

Finally, in the spring of 53 Crassus was ready. The army crossed the Euphrates in good order, but failed to find anyone to fight. Days passed without a sign of life – only the oppressive heat. At last a cluster of hoof prints were spotted, but they wheeled off into the desert and disappeared. Crassus' best lieutenant, a man named Cassius Longinus, begged his commander not to follow, but Crassus plunged ahead.

At first this determination seemed to pay off. The Parthian army was not far off, and the Romans were eager to finally come to grips with the enemy. The Parthians, however, refused to engage. They were among the finest riders of the ancient world and could fire arrows both advancing and, far more destructively, retreating[107]. All day long they wore the Romans down, charging close enough to discharge their bolts, and then retreating whenever the Romans advanced.

Driven half insane by the merciless sun, the discipline of the parched Romans began to break down. Publius tried to force the issue by leading his Gauls in pursuit of the retreating Parthians, but he was massacred. His severed head was thrown at Crassus' feet, along with jeers and the promise that the same fate awaited all of them.

Somehow, the Romans managed to pull back to the nearby city of Carrhae, but Crassus' spirit was broken. When the Parthians invited him to a parley, he unhesitatingly went. It turned out to be a ruse, and he was immediately murdered. A fewlegionnaires under the capable command of Cassius Longinus managed to make it back to Rome, but the rest were either killed or captured. It was the greatest single defeat Rome had suffered since the time of Hannibal.

---

[106] The Temple of Jerusalem was one of the buildings plundered.

[107] This is the source of the English phrase "a Parthian Shot" which refers to lobbing an explosive comment into a conversation as you leave it.

Twenty thousand lay butchered in the desert, ten thousand more were enslaved, and – worst of all – seven eagle standards had been lost[108].

Caesar barely had time to absorb this news before the same fate nearly overtook him. His greatest ally in Gaul had always been Gallic disunity. The natural tribal animosities had made it relatively simple to impose Roman authority over the whole province, but in the late winter of 53, a remarkable figure appeared that threatened to undo all of it. He was a Gallic nobleman named Vercingetorix, who provided a charisma and leadership that had hitherto been lacking. Despite the heavy snows and biting cold, he managed to unite nearly all the tribes in northern and central Gaul into a vast alliance.

Caesar was in a terrible position. He was cut off from most of his troops, separated by the Alps and miles of hostile territory. He had one legion on hand loaned by Pompey, and virtually no support anywhere in Gaul. Most commanders would have thrown in the towel; Caesar immediately sprang into action.

Traveling in disguise with only a small escort, he crossed the Alps, traversing passes choked by more than six and a half feet of snow, and managed to make contact with six of his legions in the north. The daring exploit raised spirits, but conditions were desperate. Vercingetorix had implemented a scorched earth policy and Caesar's men were running out of supplies.

Leaving an able officer named Decimus Brutus to guard his camp, Caesar went off in search of supplies. The town of Orleans provided some much needed provisions, but a relieving Gallic army proved tougher than expected, and after sustaining heavy losses he was forced to retreat back to his camp. It was his first defeat in the field in six years, and it dispelled his carefully created aura of invincibility.

Now that they saw a chink in his armor, tribes that had been faithful allies since Caesar's entry to Gaul began to defect to Vercingetorix. Caesar's lieutenants begged him to abandon Gaul, but

---

[108] There were later rumors that Crassus had been taken alive to the Parthian capital and executed by having molten gold poured down his throat. His head, at least, made that trip. The Parthian king was celebrating a wedding by watching a production of a play by Euripides. Someone threw the head on stage and a quick-thinking actor picked it up and used it as a prop.

although at a low ebb, Caesar never wavered. Let all of Gaul unite against him. If his enemies were foolish enough to reveal themselves, it would only give him an opportunity to crush all of them at once. The Roman beast was wounded, but it still had fangs.

With the campaigning season coming to an end, Vercingetorix retired to his stronghold of Alesia, north of present-day Dijon. Instead of taking the opportunity to retreat, Caesar immediately followed him.

The move was certainly daring. Alesia's defenses had never been successfully stormed, and Vercingetorix had a month's supply of food inside. He also had a larger army than Caesar and knew the surrounding countryside intimately.

But Caesar had no intention of attacking the enemy. If Vercingetorix wanted to hide, Caesar would trap him in his own lair. He erected a massive palisade some fifteen miles long to surround the fortress. As the days passed and food supplies began to dwindle, Vercingetorix expelled non-combatants from Alesia. Women and children came streaming out, accompanied by those too old, sick, or wounded to fight. When they approached the Roman lines, Caesar refused to let them pass, forcing Vercingetorix to choose between dividing his supplies or watching his own people starve. Neither side budged. Many of the refugees resorted to eating grass to survive, and even begged the Romans to accept them as slaves, but were greeted with pitiless silence, and slowly starved to death.

Vercingetorix was spared the same fate when news arrived that a quarter of a million Gauls were closing in. Caesar, who was running short of food himself, barely had time to build a second, outward-facing wall before they arrived. An attack was immediately launched. Wave after wave of Gauls hurled themselves at the Roman defenses, scrabbling up the steep sides and clawing their way over.

The Romans survived that first day by the skin of their teeth. They were now caught between two armies, both of which vastly outnumbered their own. The Gallic forces were also in communication with each other, and were able to coordinate their attacks. This meant that Caesar had to split his forces and fend off assaults both in front and behind.

The first day, for all its ferocity, had merely been a probing exercise. At some point in the fighting, the Gauls had discovered a weakness in the Roman defenses. There was a hill overlooking the wall to the north of Alesia, and it was defended by two bruised legions. A charge down the hill by the majority of the Gallic forces would quickly penetrate the wall, and once inside it would be a bloodbath.

The assault was launched at dawn, inaugurated by the blood-curdling screams of Gallic warriors. The trench that had been hastily dug was immediately filled up as thousands of bellowing men hurled themselves over the palisades. Vercingetorix led a furious assault from the other side, hoping to draw off any relief.

Gallic warriors from both sides attached hooks to the wooden beams that made up the walls and tried to pull them down. After several hours, some watchtowers collapsed, along with parts of the palisade. The Roman line buckled but somehow held, and suddenly the legionnaires started cheering. There, behind the invading Gauls was the fluttering red cape of Caesar.

Throughout the day he had been galloping along the line shouting encouragement wherever the defenses were under the most stress. He had also kept his cavalry in reserve, waiting for the right moment to throw them into the fray. When he saw Gallic troops starting to appear on the ramparts, he led his cavalry behind the massive Gallic force and abruptly charged down the hill taking them completely by surprise. The carnage was terrible. Caught between the wall and the trampling hooves of the cavalry, the Gauls could think only of escape. What had begun as an assault turned into a bloody rout.

Vercingetorix, laboring on the other side of the walls, heard the agonized screams and knew that something had gone terribly wrong. He retreated back to his fortress, but knew he was beaten. The next morning he rode out proudly, dressed in his finest armor, and prostrated himself at Caesar's feet.

The fortress itself was spared, but the troops inside were given to Caesar's legionnaires as slaves, and Vercingetorix was hauled off to Rome to await Caesar's triumph. Although there were still some pockets of resistance to mop up, the war was effectively over.

Not even his most inveterate enemy could deny that this was due entirely to Caesar's genius. Outnumbered by two armies, running critically short of supplies, Caesar had outfought both of them at the same time. Through it all he had never panicked or outwardly wavered in his confidence. To his frightened soldiers, facing impossible odds, he had offered only calm, steady leadership. It was a remarkable achievement.

There was another year of sporadic revolts, but these were only the death throes of Gallic freedom. Without a leader like Vercingetorix the Gauls had no one to unite them and any efforts to make war were increasingly half-hearted. Sensing that the last rebels were at the breaking point, Caesar employed brutality with surgical precision. After taking one rebellious city, he had the hands of every one who had taken part in its defense lopped off as a warning not to try his patience.

The tactic worked. This time peace took root and Gaul would remain a settled province for the next three hundred years. There were no further revolts, even during the chaos of the civil wars ahead. The benefits to Rome were immense. Gaul was nearly twice the size of Italy, and the tax revenue alone was staggering[109]. There was also no longer the constant threat of a Gallic invasion. Caesar had found greatness, and was at last a true rival of Pompey. As Cicero flamboyantly put it, he had made the Alps irrelevant. The only defense Rome needed was Caesar himself.

But this came at an immense price in lives. Eight hundred cities had been stormed, and more than three hundred tribes had been subdued. There were corpses everywhere. According to Caesar's hyperbolic estimates, he had killed a million Gauls, enslaved the same amount, and left what remained alone[110].

---

[109] According to Suetonius, Caesar added about 32,000 miles in circumference to Roman territory and forty million sesterces to the treasury.

[110] Cato accused him of war crimes and suggested that he should be turned over to the natives to face justice.

In the long run, however, Gaul prospered under Roman governance and became the main channel through which Greco-Roman culture was transmitted to northern Europe. In trying to win a war, Caesar had unwittingly founded the roots of French civilization.

Chapter 17

DICTATORSHIP IN THE AIR

"In peacetime... it is most important to back the side that is in the
right – but in times of war, the strongest".

- Caelius

There was another, more bitter cost to Gaul's conquest that was
both personal and political. In the decade that Caesar had been
away from Rome his mother, daughter and grandchild had all died.
The loss of his mother, Aurelia, would have been a terrible blow – she
had always been an anchor in his life – but the death of his daughter
in childbirth was potentially explosive.

Julia was his only legitimate child, and her marriage to Pompey
had gone a long way toward sealing the alliance between the two men.
By all accounts Pompey had loved her fiercely, to the point where he
was gently mocked for it[111].

Personal feelings aside, her death could hardly have come at
a worse time. The death of Crassus had changed the relationship
between the other two triumvirs more profoundly than anyone
suspected. The relationships of all three triumvirs had always been
motivated by a certain amount of paranoia. Each had feared that the
other two might gang up on them; the only real option – as Caesar
repeatedly pointed out – had been to work together. Now that basic
political calculus had changed. With only two great men there was
no longer an obvious benefit to cooperation. What was the point of
strengthening a potential rival?

If Caesar had grown great in Gaul, Pompey had grown even greater
by staying in Rome. While his colleagues had marched off in pursuit

---

[111] A contemporary noted incredulously that Pompey hadn't had an affair
while he was married to Julia.

of military glory, he had announced that he would be governing his province – Spain – by proxy. His detractors whispered that he was growing soft, unwilling to leave a young wife and his comfortable mansion, but he ignored them. Instead, of campaigning he spent his time designing a massive tribute to himself on the Campus Martius.

Subtlety wasn't Pompey's style. A sprawling complex of buildings was erected inside an immaculately landscaped park. Works of art plundered from each region Pompey had conquered were delicately arranged along shaded walks, and marbled porticoes led to auditoriums adorned by splashing fountains. There was a new curia for emergency meetings of the Senate, a new house for himself, and a large temple to Venus Victrix[112].

The *pièce de résistance*, however, was a theater, the first permanent one ever built in Rome. It was also the largest one ever constructed in the city, with space for over forty thousand spectators. Towering over the stage and seating area were fourteen statues, each representing a foreign nation that Pompey had conquered.

The fact that all of this was built overshadowing the ovile – the voting pens of the Roman people – could hardly be missed. From now on elections would be held quite literally in Pompey's shadow. Senators were provided with the same message. Inside of the new meeting space he had made for them was the most exquisite statue of all. A larger-than-life one of himself gazing down imperiously at them[113].

By the beginning of 52 BC, the senators had gotten the message. The street fighting between Milo and Clodius had reached fever pitch during the elections at the end of 53, when the presiding official was knocked out with a brick. This was followed by riots that not even Clodius' assassination – ironically at an altar to the Bona Dea – could

---

[112] Theaters were frowned upon because they eroded the moral fiber of the people. Pompey cleverly sidestepped this by explaining that it was actually a gift to his patron goddess, Venus the Victorious – who also happened to be Rome's patron as well. All performances would be dedicated to her for the continued protection and glory of Rome. Not even Cato could object to that.

[113] The nine and a half foot statue of Pompey currently in the Villa Arconati, about three miles north of Milan, is probably this one.

quench[114]. His outraged supporters brought his corpse back to the Forum, and the resulting funeral pyre engulfed both the Senate chamber and the nearby law courts – a fitting dénouement for such a talented troublemaker.

With Caesar away, there was only one person who could restore order. Pompey was made sole consul – a flagrantly illegal position – and tasked with saving the Republic. He had always been a brilliant organizer, and this task was perfectly suited to his skills. The gangs infesting Rome were no match for his veterans. Within a month order had been restored.

The applause was unanimous. When Pompey selected a colleague to finish out his term, thereby dispelling any fears of tyranny, even Cato had to admit that he had behaved impeccably. He was cheered in the streets, and lauded in the Senate. Patricians who had mocked him behind his back for years tripped over themselves to congratulate him. It was the moment he had been waiting for all his life. He was the most powerful, beloved figure in Rome, and everybody knew it.

In Gaul, Caesar knew it too. Searching for some way to keep their alliance intact, he offered his grandniece, Octavia, as a new bride[115]. Pompey barely considered it before refusing. He could do far better than a Julian now. He was the most eligible bachelor in Rome, and had his pick of blue-blooded ladies. He chose Cornelia, the fabulously well-connected widow of Publius Crassus[116]. At long last, Pompey had been accepted into the rarefied air of Rome's upper crust.

This was a blow to Caesar, although just how severe was not yet clear. Pompey's triumph undid the need for a partnership in the first place. His troops were loyal and his position in Rome was unassailable. What could Caesar possibly give him that he couldn't take for himself?

---

[114] It would not be the end of the family's influence. Clodius' daughter married Augustus.
[115] She was the sister of the future emperor Augustus, and would eventually marry Mark Antony.
[116] Cornelia was directly related to the Scipio who had defeated Hannibal. She was less than half Pompey's age, and was his fifth wife.

This didn't mean that he was Caesar's enemy, just that an alliance between them was no longer something that could be taken for granted. Inevitably, however, he began to drift toward Cato and those august senators whose acceptance he had always so desperately wanted. Encouraged by his obvious ambivalence, the conservative attacks on Caesar began to grow bolder. In 51, a Gaul who had been granted citizenship by Caesar was seized and the sitting consul had him publicly flogged without a trial. Pompey didn't raise a finger in the man's defense, although he did reluctantly veto a stronger measure which directly attacked his fellow triumvir.

Caesar's many enemies were now openly sharpening their knives. His term of office would expire in 50 BC along with his legal protection. If he appeared in Rome as a civilian he would be dragged in front of a kangaroo court and would be lucky to escape with exile – Cato publicly promised as much. Caesar's only option was to get elected to another post before his current term ended, but as an active general he was forbidden from entering Rome without first resigning his command.

His solution to this dilemma was to ask the Senate to allow him to stand for elections in absentia. All eyes turned to Pompey. The year before, he had amended the law so that candidates had to personally appear to be considered for office. Would he create a loophole for his colleague, or openly break with Caesar?

The choice was agonizing. Pompey was perfectly happy with the way things were, and vacillated between Cato – who wanted to crush Caesar at all costs – and his natural reluctance to choose between rival blocs. He still seems not to have seen Caesar as an outright enemy, and had no desire to make him one. After weeks of wavering, however, he informed the Senate that he opposed Caesar's petition.

While there was now no doubt where Pompey stood, Caesar still tried to find a political solution. Money and agents flooded into Rome in the service of his cause. Pompey responded by attempting to weaken Caesar militarily. The legions that had fallen with Crassus still hadn't been replaced, and men were needed to shore up the Syrian frontier. Pompey cunningly suggested that each of them should donate a legion to this cause. His contribution would be the legion that he had loaned to Caesar two years before, which effectively meant that Caesar would be losing two. Caesar obliged after paying each of Pompey's soldiers a hefty bonus. They may be Pompey's men, but he would make sure that they felt no ill will towards Caesar.

Pompey followed this with a bill that would force Caesar to resign his command several months before election day. This would leave plenty of time for his senatorial enemies to drag Caesar through the courts to his inevitable conviction. To drive the point home, Caesar's veterans who had been given land would be stripped of their citizenship as well. At a stroke he would neuter his rival and perhaps sow doubt in the minds of his current soldiers. Caesar, however, had weapons of his own. An amenable tribune was found and – after a hefty bribe – he vetoed Pompey's bill.

At this fateful moment, Pompey's health abruptly broke[117]. There was wild speculation that the great man was dying. Rome would be bereft of her protector and at the mercy of Caesar and his legions. Throughout the countryside sacrifices were made and prayers said for his recovery. When he finally appeared in public again, the outburst of joy was as genuine as it was overwhelming. All of Italy seemed to breathe a sigh of relief.

For Pompey, always insecure about his popularity, it was a much needed boost to his confidence. He began to show much more spine and enthusiasm for the struggle ahead. When one supporter expressed concern about Caesar's legions, Pompey haughtily told him not to worry because he merely had to "stamp his foot and soldiers will rise from the ground".

Caesar, for his part, prepared one last attempt to find a political solution. He sent one of his most able legates, Mark Antony, to Rome where he was rapidly elected as a tribune. On the surface, it was a curious choice. Antony was a relative of Caesar on his mother's side, and was considered something of a black sheep of the family. His father had died when he was only eleven, and without any paternal

---

[117] There were rumours that he was actually sulking because Caesar had wriggled through his trap.

guidance he had fallen in with a rough crowd. He had joined one of Coldius' street gangs, and became famous for drunken escapades. Crushing debt had forced him out of Rome, and eventually into the army.

He may have been debauched, but he was also quick thinking and brutally effective. He had commanded a cavalry unit at Alesia, and had been instrumental in the final charge that broke the Gauls. His courage was as indisputable as his appetite. If Pompey wanted a fight, Caesar would send a brawler.

Antony arrived just in time. In December of 50, one of the consuls appeared at Pompey's villa with a sword conspicuously in his hand. A huge crowd gathered as the official theatrically handed the weapon to Pompey and requested that he use it against Caesar[118]. Pompey bowed his head gravely and responded that he would if no other way to peace was found. He then turned around with a flourish and disappeared to begin raising an army.

The fact that Pompey was now gathering troops to attack a legally appointed official – a flagrantly illegal activity – wasn't worth protesting. With Pompey's forces beginning to enter the city, there was little point in raising legal objections. Most of Caesar's supporters began fleeing Rome to avoid prosecution.

The mood in the city was tense. Most citizens, whatever they thought of the principals, had no desire to experience a civil war. Some, like Cicero were still trying to keep a foot in both camps and were terrified about the future of the Republic. Each day that passed, however, made neutrality more impossible.

On January 1, 49, Mark Antony tried one last time to prevent a civil war. At an emergency meeting of the Senate, he announced that Caesar was willing to resign his commission and disband his armies if Pompey pledged to do the same thing. For a brief moment, there seemed to be a ray of hope. This was eminently sensible – both sides could save face and untold bloodshed could be prevented.

---

[118] This was doubly cutting because the consul was married to one of Caesar's nieces.

Some senators began to waver, but Cato stiffened them. He had Antony's proposal suppressed and issued an ultimatum demanding that Caesar dismiss his forces or be declared an enemy of the Republic. Antony vetoed this immediately and dryly warned Cato that Caesar could mobilize his veterans faster than Pompey his raw levies. With that he turned on his heel and left. There was no further point in negotiating.

Six days later, a bill was signed giving Pompey emergency powers. A warning was issued to Caesar's tribunes that the government couldn't guarantee their safety. Mark Antony and the few remaining Caesarians slipped out of the city disguised as slaves as the first of Pompey's troops marched in, and sped toward Caesar's camp in Ravenna where he was waiting with a single legion.

Caesar took the news that he was now an outlaw stoically. Not wanting to tip off any potential spies, he continued going through his normal routine as if nothing at all had happened. He spent several hours watching gladiators practice, and went over plans for a new training facility he wanted to build. When evening came, he took a bath and then went to a dinner party where he chatted calmly with the guests. A few hours into this he excused himself, asking his fellow diners to wait until he returned[119].

Outside, he ordered the 13th Legion to march toward Italy while he dispatched orders for the rest of his troops to cross the Alps and join the invasion. Then, borrowing a team of mules from a nearby bakery, he overtook his troops as they reached the Rubicon river. He paused on the bank, staring for a long time at the little bridge that spanned it, feeling the immense weight of his decision. This insignificant stream was the pomerium, the sacred boundary dividing Gaul from Italy. If he crossed it, untold thousands of his fellow citizens would die.

The seemingly trivial act of crossing a river would proclaim his intention of taking Rome by force, and his enemies would have no choice but to declare him an enemy of the state. All the horrors of a civil war would be unleashed – not just on his homeland, but across

---

[119] We know this as one of the dinner guests that night was the Roman historian Sallust.

three continents. Every inhabitant of the Republic would be forced to pick a side. Families would be ripped apart, and brother would kill brother.

But if he refused to cross the river, he would spend the rest of his life in exile. His accomplishments would be for nothing, his name would be erased, and his immediate family would be persecuted.

Already the odds seemed stacked against him. He had a single legion against the overwhelming resources of Pompey and the Senate. The moment he crossed the Rubicon he would be the aggressor, already behind in the propaganda war to persuade hearts and minds. But what was the alternative? A Caesar without honour was no Caesar at all.

Ever the gambler, he quoted a line from the Greek poet Menander: Iacta alea est – "The die is cast!" Then he galloped across the bridge.

Chapter 18

THE CIVIL WAR

"Fortune favours the bold"

- Virgil

A single legion crossing the Rubicon split the Roman Republic in two. Every citizen now had a terrible choice to make: support one of the two factions or try to remain neutral and hope the victor was forgiving. This wasn't just a civilian decision. Caesar was well aware of how much he was asking of his soldiers. To follow him was to become an outlaw, to forfeit property and to expose one's family to death or worse. They needed to be reassured that right was on their side.

Caesar took this task seriously. Mark Antony, still dressed as a slave, was brought out in front of the13th Legion. This was how Pompey and Cato treated those who had faithfully served the state. They had tamed Gaul and taught the barbarians beyond the Rhine and the great Ocean to fear Rome. Their reward for this great service was to be vilified and spit upon. Murmurs of surprise at seeing Antony so shabbily dressed turned into shouts of outrage. Cato's allies had already tried to disenfranchise Caesar's veterans; an assault on Caesar's honour was an assault on them.

The 13th roared their approval of the crossing. They owed everything to Caesar. Not only had he nearly doubled their salaries, but all their future prospects of land and rights depended on his ability to push them through politically. A government dominated by men like Pompey and Cato was unthinkable.

The rest of the Roman world found the choice of who to support a good deal harder than the 13th Legion. Virtually all of the nobility had family in both camps. Brutus, for example, was the son of

Caesar's favourite mistress, but he had been raised by Cato. Further complicating the choice was the fact that Pompey had killed Brutus' father, and he was extremely reluctant to have anything to do with the man. Eventually, Cato's influence won out, and Brutus took up arms with his father's murderer.

Most Romans seem to have been ambivalent. Pompey and Caesar were two of the Republic's most admired men, and both had brought immense glory to Rome. The majority of the populace had no real stake in the fight, didn't want a war, and just wanted to be left alone.

It was also hard to decide immediately which of the two was stronger. Caesar had twelve veteran legions with a proven track record, but they were all under strength, and with the exception of a single legion, were north of the Alps. Pompey, on the other hand, had nearly unlimited troops, but they were scattered around the Mediterranean. Spain, North Africa, and the East were awash with resources, but it would take time to gather them. Meanwhile, he only had two legions with him in Italy.

In the long run, the safe bet seemed to be Pompey. The great man had already issued a call for recruits and men were trickling into Rome. These could train through the winter and when added to the seven full-strength Pompeian legions in Spain and the untold numbers from the East, would crush Caesar. The only question was how much time would elapse before that happened.

But time was one thing that Caesar didn't give Pompey. News that he had crossed the Rubicon was greeted with shock and outright disbelief. Was he mad advancing with a single legion in winter? Pompey's bluff had been called and the bravado collapsed like a popped balloon. His two legions were of dubious loyalty – both had seen service with Caesar in Gaul – and he had no wish to test his raw recruits. His strength was in the East; if Caesar wanted Rome so badly he could have it temporarily. Pompey bolted for southern Italy, advising anyone "who preferred liberty to tyranny" to follow him.

Not everyone shared Pompey's wariness. The flight from Rome wasn't exactly the robust leadership that had been promised, and several patricians ignored Pompey's instructions. Chief among these was a pompous senator named Lucius Domitius Ahenobarbus who decided to teach the rebel a lesson. Ahenobarbus had been a staunch opponent of Caesar for most of his career, and had been informed that Caesar's soldiers were on the brink of mutiny. Armed with this bit of wishful thinking, he advanced north and camped out in the town of Corfinum. At the sight of Caesar's army, however, he completely lost his head and tried to run away. He was captured by his own troops who promptly turned him over to Caesar and surrendered.

It was a perfect opportunity for Caesar to broadcast his intentions to all of Italy, and he made good use of it. Summoning Ahenobarbus and all of the captured officers, he reminded them of his past service to Rome, his generosity to many of them, and offered a careful defense of his crossing of the Rubicon. He then released all of them, including Ahenobarbus who was furiously demanding to be killed[120]. The captured troops took an oath of loyalty to Caesar and joined his army.

This clemency was undoubtedly sincere but it was also tremendous propaganda. What better way to reassure a worried populace that was expecting a bloodbath than to show mercy? As Caesar himself said, "History proves that by practicing cruelty you earn nothing but hatred".

This policy paid off immediately. Every city or town he approached in Italy threw open its gates. There was no plundering, no proscriptions, and no executions, so why should they resist? Even Picenum, the birthplace of Pompey and the heart of his Italian lands, surrendered with barely a token resistance.

As Caesar swept down the Italian peninsula, the mood in Pompey's camp became increasingly fractious. One senator sarcastically asked him if perhaps now was a good time to 'stamp his foot' and make those soldiers appear. But Pompey had no intention of defending Italy. Despite all of his bluster, he was in a weak position and knew it. The vast majority of his veterans were settled in Spain and Asia,

---

[120] He also returned Ahenobarbus' captured war chest to underline that he had not crossed the Rubicon to enrich himself. Ahenobarbus immediately rejoined Pompey's army.

and even under the best circumstances they couldn't possibly reach Rome before Caesar. The forces he had in Italy represented only a tiny fraction of his strength, and it would be foolish to risk a showdown before he was absolutely ready. A more natural place to make a stand was Greece, which was within easy reach of his forces already in the field, and didn't require a dangerous mountain or water crossing to reach.

The plan to abandon Italy was unpopular, and was made more so by Pompey's unhelpful decision to keep it to himself. Only when he had reached the port city of Brundisium, the main crossing point to Greece, did he bother to share his plans with the rest of his command staff. There was predictable outrage – particularly by senators who had fled to Pompey in the belief that he would quickly beat Caesar – but by then there was no other alternative.

Since there wasn't time to build a fleet, Pompey commandeered every merchant ship and fishing vessel within miles of Brundisium. Just as he was loading the first troops on these makeshift transports, Caesar showed up.

Pompey's genius had always been in organization, and in this first direct clash he performed brilliantly. Caesar had his troops construct a pontoon barrier to trap Pompey's ships in the harbour while harassing those trying to board. After a sustained effort, however, Pompey's improvised fleet was able to break through at night and evacuate the entire group supposedly without a single casualty.

There was no chance for Caesar to immediately follow. Pompey had seized most ships in the area and it would take weeks to find enough to make a crossing. Instead he turned his army around and headed for Rome.

The last Roman general who had entered Rome with an army had initiated a bloodbath, but Caesar had something very different in mind. His enemies had branded him an outlaw, and a normally functioning government would go a long way towards undermining that claim. He shrewdly made it known that he considered all who were not actively against him, for him[121]. This meant that most could remain safely neutral without risking their lives.

His attempts to convene the Senate, however, were disappointing. Most of the body had either fled with Pompey or to their country villas to wait out events, and weren't about to return to Rome when Caesar summoned them. Despite barely having a quorum, he soldiered on, detailing the injustice done to him, and reassuring them that he had only proceeded out of necessity. For those who still feared he would be a new Sulla, he pointed to the fact that he had made himself master over all of Italy without spilling a drop of blood.

There was some muted applause, but most of the senators sat on their hands. They were certainly glad that there were no proscriptions, but it was still unclear what Caesar would do, and Pompey was lurking out there with his endless legions. It would take more than a nice speech to turn them into supporters.

The soft touch encouraged defiance. When he announced that he would be confiscating the treasury to fund the war effort, one of the tribunes bravely vetoed it, quoting a law that forbade removing public money. Caesar retorted that there was a time for law and a time for weapons. When the man persisted, Caesar warned that war wasn't the time for free speech.

The tribune refused to take the hint. He followed Caesar to the treasury, and when the doors were forced open he tried to physically prevent the general from entering[122]. At this Caesar's patience finally snapped and he threatened to kill the man, adding menacingly that for him this was "more distasteful to say than to do".

The truth was that Caesar didn't have much time. Pompey had seven legions in Spain that might descend on Italy – or Gaul – at any point, and Pompey himself was in the East gathering strength. Every month that Caesar delayed attacking him was another month to train and equip that vast army.

---

[121] Pompey, by contrast, had said that all who were not actively for him were against him.

[122] The consuls had barred the doors and taken the only key with them to Pompey.

He stayed in Rome less than three weeks. Before most of the populace had gotten used to his arrival he was marching toward Spain, joking that he was going to fight an army without a general. He left a noble named Marcus Lepidus behind to govern Rome, and Mark Antony to watch over Italy. If things went well, he said, he would be back to fight a general without an army.

Chapter 19

FINDING POMPEY

"To make a path by havoc was his joy."

-Lucan

There was no one who could move quite like Caesar in a rush. He covered more than twelve hundred miles in twenty-seven days and hit the Pompeian forces like a thunderbolt. He had joked that his enemies didn't have a leader, but the truth was that they had too many. Overall command was divided between three men: a tired veteran in his sixties, the scholar Varro, and a former consul whose only talent appears to have been showing off his calves. Needless to say, none of them was remotely capable of standing up to Caesar.

This basic truth was widely known among the Pompeian soldiers themselves. Caesar's reputation spoke for itself, and their own commanders didn't inspire much confidence. One legion under the command of Varro simply switched sides the moment Caesar arrived, and the rest were manoeuvered onto a hillside without food or water. After a few token days of resistance, an unconditional surrender was signed. In just over a month, Caesar had broken all effective resistance without fighting a major battle. As usual, he pardoned everybody. The three commanders fled to Pompey to continue the fight, but many of the troops joined his army.

The only thing that marred the victory was a short incident near Cordoba. During a minor skirmish, Caesar had collapsed, falling to the ground with what Plutarch called "a distemper of the head"[123]. It was the first of several attacks which he would suffer over the next two years, which would leave him insensate and weak. The brush with mortality seems only to have quickened the pace of the vigorous fifty-four year old. Time was running out.

Any hopes that the war would be short were dashed once Caesar returned to Rome. In his absence, two of his lieutenants had suffered humiliating defeats. The first, a legate named Curio had invaded North Africa in an attempt to capture Cato, who had established an alliance with a native king. The battle had gone poorly from the start, and both Curio and his two legions had been wiped out. At roughly the same time, one of Mark Antony's brothers lost another two legions in what is now modern Croatia[124].

More worryingly, Caesar was now faced with the first mutiny of his career. The Ninth Legion had been with him for over a decade, and was one of the original units he had commanded as governor of Spain. They had marched with him over the Rhine and across the Ocean, and many began to wonder if he would ever stop. Even the sharpest sword, they grumbled, got worn out with enough use.

The dissent was fanned by a few ringleaders who pointed out that Caesar's policy of clemency had robbed them of the usual chances to plunder, and that the promised bonuses to compensate for this had yet to be paid. Now was the time to act. The threat of Pompey gave them the leverage they needed.

The situation was alarming enough that those around Caesar began to urge him to give in to the demands and make peace with Pompey while there was still time. Instead, he travelled immediately to the mutinous camp and faced them down in person.

---

[123] Although the ancient consensus was epilepsy, there has been considerable discussion about what Caesar actually suffered from. Suetonius describes "sudden fainting fits", and Appian writes of "convulsions". Caesar himself may have encouraged the diagnosis of epilepsy since many considered it a sign of divine possession. Two paleopathologists – Drs. Galassi and Ashrafian – have recently made a persuasive argument that Caesar suffered from mini-strokes instead.

[124] Several senators – including Cicero – took advantage of Caesar's absence in Spain to join Pompey.

The sight of their general had a sobering effect. It was one thing to grumble to fellow soldiers, and quite another to have Caesar standing there. His first words to them – "citizens" – reduced them to tears. They had always been "fellows", his brothers-in-arms. The special bond had been broken. They had been dishonourably discharged and were unworthy to be called his men. The mood abruptly switched. Those in the front ranks began shouting, begging for forgiveness and the opportunity to demonstrate their loyalty.

Caesar let the noise built to a crescendo before raising his hand. He would allow them to remain under arms, but would decimate them as a punishment. After more cries, this was eventually commuted to twelve men. Lots were drawn and – in a carefully rigged result – the main instigators of the mutiny were selected. For the rest of the war, the Ninth Legion fought with particular distinction.

The entire episode underscored Caesar's need to come to grips with Pompey, and he moved quickly to settle his affairs in Rome. His lieutenant, Lepidus, had conveniently introduced a bill making him dictator, allowing Caesar to push through whatever acts he wanted. In a flurry of activity, he recalled all exiles, forgave most debts, and arranged for his election as consul. Having done this, he resigned his dictatorship – after only eleven days – and immediately left Rome for southern Italy where his transports were waiting.

Pompey, meanwhile, had made good use of his time by virtually emptying the East of troops. He seemed everywhere at once, organizing supplies, concluding alliances, and even training with his men. This last in particular earned him rave reviews. Though well past middle age and more than a decade removed from his last battle, he was surprisingly vibrant. It was noted approvingly that he could throw a javelin further than most soldiers and ride a horse at breakneck speed. Any lingering doubt over his fitness was resolved.

He was kept current on affairs in Rome by a steady stream of deserters who informed him that Caesar was intending to cross to Greece from the heel of Italy. Pompey gave command of a fleet of five hundred warships to Caesar's old nemesis, Bibulus, to prevent this.

Caesar had further problems to contend with. It was now January of 48, and winter storms were starting to make the water treacherous. Caesar was also chronically short of transports – a consequence of moving so quickly. At most, he could only fit half of his army onto the ships at a time, which meant braving stormy, infested waters twice.

Fortunately, Caesar's luck held. Crossing the Aegean in winter was so risky that Bibulus had effectively stopped patrolling the sea. After landing safely in Epirus,[125] Caesar launched an attack on Pompey's main supply center of Dyrrachium without waiting for the other half of his army to arrive[126].

The city was too well defended to be taken – Pompey's force was twice the size of Caesar's – but the attack unnerved the Pompeians. While Bibulus swore to redouble his blockade and execute everyone he captured, Pompey's troops felt the need to take a public oath to remain faithful to their general.

By now the winter had arrived in force, and both sides dug in. As the weeks dragged on, Pompey's army continued to grow, while Caesar remained stranded with half his men. There was no word from Mark Antony who was in charge of the crossing, and Caesar's lone attempt to establish contact personally failed when he was forced back by strong winds.

The spring, however, brought good news. Bibulus, exhausted by his efforts at sea, succumbed to disease, and Mark Antony arrived with the bulk of the army. His time in Italy hadn't exactly been spent covering himself with glory – his habit of binge drinking and wild partying had cemented his debauched reputation – but his appearance boosted everyone's confidence[127].

Now back at full force, Caesar immediately moved on Pompey's supply center, but Pompey got word of it and beat him there. Caesar arrived to find Pompey's army building a defensive wall that

---

[125] A few ships were intercepted by Bibulus. He was so enraged at missing his enemy that he had the crews burned alive.

[126] This city – now Durrës in modern-day Albania – was the western terminus of the Via Egnatia, the second-most important road in the Roman world which ran for nearly seven hundred miles to the city of Byzantium.

[127] On one occasion he dressed up as the god of wine and – presumably inebriated – drove around Rome in a chariot drawn by two lions.

stretched fifteen miles around the city. Undaunted, he had his men erect palisades surrounding Pompey in turn, trapping the larger army inside.

For the first time, the full armies were now facing each other, but neither side wanted to attack. Instead, they settled into a siege. Pompey was supplied by sea with lines stretching all the way to Asia, but food quickly became a problem for Caesar. Bread was so scarce that his men began mixing local roots with milk and baking the vile result into a barely edible lump.

This "bread" soon became a point of pride – a symbol of how far Caesar's men were willing to go for victory. Before long they were throwing loaves of it into Pompey's camp, taunting the softness of their enemies. When he was brought a sample of this, Pompey was horrified, wondering aloud if they were fighting men or beasts. Adding to his unease was the fact that his tightly packed camp was beginning to suffer from disease and a lack of water.

For once, Pompey was the first to make a move, launching a furious assault against the section of walls manned by the disgraced Ninth Legion. The unit redeemed itself with a spirited defense. One centurion kept fighting with wounds to both arms and legs, somehow still wielding a shield with a hundred and twenty arrows embedded in it[128].

Even with this heroic effort, however, part of the wall was overrun. Mark Antony's timely arrival stabilized the situation, but Caesar was forced to withdraw, leaving part of his fortifications in enemy hands. Rather than try to retake it, he launched a counter-attack on one of Pompey's forts, hoping to catch him by surprise. His men faltered, however, and the line broke. Pompey's forces surged forward, nearly catching Caesar in the rout.

It was the worst defeat of his career. The failed assault had cost him nearly a thousand men, and thirty-two of his standards had been captured by the enemy. Far worse was the damage to his reputation.

---

[128] After the battle, the survivors picked up over thirty thousand arrows that had been fired at the Ninth Legion.

The aura of invincibility had been punctured, and his entire army was near panic. If Pompey attacked now, all would be lost.

Incredibly, Pompey didn't. Not wanting to blunder into an ambush or one of Caesar's ruses, he called a halt to his advance without even testing the lines. Caesar couldn't believe his luck. That man, he said, doesn't know how to win a war.

Caesar spent the afternoon encouraging his men. Pompey, hoping to unnerve them, executed all of his prisoners in view of Caesar's lines, but this had the opposite effect. The legion that had been routed demanded to be punished for their failure, and the entire army begged to attack immediately.

While Caesar doubtlessly appreciated the sentiment, he wasn't about to waste his strength in another attack. Pompey's position was too entrenched to be dislodged, and – since part of the encircling wall had fallen – there was no point in trying to maintain a siege.

Pompey's army awoke the next morning to find the walls facing them deserted. Caesar had fled.

Chapter 20

SUNSET AT PHARSALUS

"Fortune decreed the doom which swept the ruins of a world away"

- Lucan

News of Caesar's defeat travelled faster than his army. There was a growing sense that he was finished and the first city he reached in Thessaly refused even to trade with him. This was a worrying development for an army that had to live off the land, so as a warning Caesar sacked it, allowing his men to commit atrocities inside[129].

The brutality solved his supply issues, but only confirmed the feeling that he was growing desperate. Pompey's camp could feel it too. Their great enemy was on the run and victory was in the air. One more push and the war would be over.

The only real question was how exactly to proceed. Some wanted to reoccupy Rome, others argued for a decisive blow to crush Caesar while he was wounded. The only person who seemed not to share the general optimism was Pompey himself. He knew exactly how dangerous Caesar's veterans were and was determined not to pursue him until he was completely ready. Two Syrian legions were still en route – why risk a battle before they arrived? He had more money, more supplies, and more native allies. The longer he waited, the weaker Caesar would become.

This was an astute judgment – Pompey's position was superior to Caesar's in every conceivable way – but the waiting infuriated his senatorial allies. They began to refer to Pompey as 'Agamemnon', the leader of the Greeks at Troy whose vanity nearly cost them the war.

---

[129] Many leading officials of the city committed suicide rather than fall into Caesar's hands – a radical departure for a man famous for his clemency.

A rumour began circulating that he was purposefully prolonging the struggle to underscore his pre-eminence. How else to explain the failure to pursue a clearly weakened Caesar?

As tension and mistrust rose, the bickering increased. Many of the senators who had joined Pompey began arguing over which posts they would get after Caesar was defeated[130]. They began picking out new villas near the Forum – currently owned by Caesar's supporters – and even dispatched agents to buy them. Others began planning how they would punish both Caesar's supporters as well as those who had stayed neutral[131].

Of course none of this would happen if Pompey didn't get his act together and finish the war. The more he dragged his feet, the greater the pressure became. Cicero compared him to a hen being ruthlessly pecked, unable to use his own judgment.

Finally, in early August, after a month of tortured waiting, the Syrian legions arrived. Pompey gave the orders to march, and the army lumbered south to where Caesar was waiting in Greece.

The two armies met at Pharsalus, on the southern edge of the plain of Thessaly. According to at least one antique tradition, this was the birthplace of Achilles; a fitting place for a battle that would decide the fate of the world. To the west rose the Pindus mountains, separating Greece from Epirus, to the south was the Enipeus river where Caesar was camped.

Even now, Pompey didn't want to engage. He had evidence that Caesar's army was suffering from both the plague and a severe shortage of food. Each day that passed weakened them. He could see it in Caesar's increasingly desperate attempts to goad him into a battle. All he had to do was wait and time would do the rest. But the senators who had joined him couldn't see this[132]. To them, Pompey was playing politics, allowing their enemy to keep slipping away. They

---

[130] The dispute over who would get Caesar's title of Pontifex Maximus nearly resulted in blows.

[131] The irony was that Cato and his cronies referred to themselves as "boni" – good men. Cicero wryly commented that apart from their cause there was nothing good about them at all.

[132] The exception was Cato who applauded this plan on the grounds that it would save Roman lives.

had Caesar now, and they weren't about to let Pompey get in the way of their glorious victory. Faced with this unrelenting pressure, Pompey gave in. Orders were given to move into position and attack the following day.

That night, the mood in Pompey's camp was festive. Senators decorated their tents with victory bouquets and planned elaborate feasts to celebrate the coming triumph. Some, more thoughtful ones, wondered what exactly victory would mean. Cicero, writing to a friend, confessed his deep despair. This wasn't a battle to save the Republic, but to anoint a tyrant. Either way, the Republic died.

On August 9, 48 BC, the two armies took up their final positions. Caesar, who had spent the night making sacrifices to his ancestor Venus and encouraging his men, had less than half of Pompey's forces. The army facing them was immense, with over twelve client kings and a staggeringly diverse collection of allies from places as far afield as Germany and Arabia[133].

Despite the mismatch, the mood in Caesar's camp was determined. Just before the battle, he had assured his men that Pompey's star was past its zenith – a clever reminder of Pompey's boast the men don't worship the setting sun – and exhorted them to remember the oath they took to leave as conquerors or not at all. Caesar had also taken another, unusual precaution. He knew that Pompey's cavalry – usually the centerpiece of his rival's strategy – had been drawn from the nobility. He instructed his men to aim their spears at the faces of their opponents, trusting that vanity would do the rest[134].

One of Caesar's men, a grizzled veteran, roared out a challenge to his comrades to follow his example, and charged forward. An entire infantry wing under the command of Mark Antony surged after him, and battle was joined.

---

[133] To reduce friendly casualties in the chaos of fighting, both sides had chosen passwords. Caesar's was "Venus the Bringer of Victory", and Pompey's was "Hercules the Unconquered".

[134] He also instructed them to ignore the allied forces who were fighting with Pompey since they were merely fighting for money. If his men could break their Roman enemies they would win the war.

The press of Pompey's forces inexorably began to push Caesar back. To avoid being outflanked, Caesar had stretched his lines until they were half as deep as Pompey's, and now they were threatening to break. Seeing them waver, Pompey sent in his heavy cavalry to finish the job, but Caesar's tactic worked. Pompey's horsemen were repulsed with heavy casualties, and they fled in disorder. Caesar, whose flashing red cloak could be seen by everyone, immediately pushed forward, charging hard into Pompey's flank and slaughtering the now unprotected archers and slingers.

Pompey's center managed to stop the rout, but the tide of the battle had turned. By midday, the Pompeian line began to splinter, and Caesar's cavalry trampled the panicked foot soldiers. From that moment on, the battle was essentially over.

Pompey made no attempt to rally his men or issue any further orders. It was, as one commentator said, as if he had forgotten that he was Pompey the Great. The moment he saw his line begin to waver, he ripped off his general's cloak and fled to his camp. He sank to the ground without saying a word and stared into the air. Only when the camp itself came under attack did he snap out of his reverie. Leaping onto the nearest horse he galloped out of the back gates and headed for the Aegean coast.

Caesar, meanwhile, was already thinking about the future. As soon as the tide of battle had turned, he had shouted for his men to spare the lives of their fellow citizens[135]. Having won it, he extended his famous clemency to all who would take it. Brutus was pardoned, as was Cassius and Cicero, and most of Pompey's soldiers joined his army[136]. Cato, of course, rejected even the thought of surrender, vowing to neither shave nor cut his hair until he was either victorious or dead. He fled to North Africa and rallied the remaining Republicans. Even Cato, however, couldn't deny the victor's magnanimity. In his report of the battle to the Senate, Caesar wrote that the best part of

---

[135] Not a single Pompeian was killed by Caesar's men after the fighting was over.

[136] Many of the men who assassinated Caesar were pardoned at Pharsalus.

his victory was in "saving the lives of citizens who had always fought against him".

The scale of the victory, and its lopsided nature, was staggering. As many as fifteen thousand men lay dead on the field, virtually all of them Pompey's soldiers[137]. Looking at the carnage, Caesar bitterly reflected on the stubbornness of his enemies. "They wanted this" he said, "they would have condemned me regardless of what I did".

His mood was undoubtedly improved by the entry into Pompey's camp where the hubris of his enemies was on full display. In contrast to Caesar who had destroyed his camp as a message that the only options were victory or death, the Pompeians had hung garlands of myrtle and laid out dining couches and tables with congratulatory flowers and bowls of wine. Caesar commandeered Pompey's tent, eating the prepared dinner off of his rival's best silver plate.

Pompey, meanwhile, was fleeing for his life. He made no attempt to re-form his forces in Greece, choosing instead to head for Egypt. This was a sensible choice. The Ptolemaic kingdom was the last vestige of Alexander the Great's empire. It was wealthy, cultured, and the only remaining independent power in the Mediterranean. Even better, its king, Ptolemy XIII, was his client. There was no better spot to rebuild his fortunes.

Caesar pursued him with his customary speed, but this time his haste nearly undid him. While crossing the Hellespont in a single ship he ran into ten Pompeian warships. He avoided capture by demanding that they surrender to him, which after a moment's hesitation they did. Caesar consented to let his troops catch up and – perhaps a bit more soberly – continued the chase[138].

Somehow managing to stay one step ahead of his pursuers, Pompey reached Pelusium, on the east side of the Nile Delta, accompanied

---

[137] Caesar claimed to have lost just two hundred men.
[138] The romantic story that Caesar visited Troy during his pursuit and gazed upon the city of his ancestors is sadly, legendary.

only by his wife, senior officers, and a few supporters[139]. There, his ship sat at anchor while formal permission to enter Ptolemaic territory was sought. The request for asylum threw the palace into an uproar. Pompey may have been an ally, but admitting him to the city would antagonize Caesar. The teenaged Ptolemy asked his closest advisor what to do."A corpse doesn't bite,"came the response.

A row boat with several Egyptians and two officers who had known Pompey for years, was dispatched, and Pompey climbed in. The officers apologized for the humble greeting, promising that there would be a more suitable welcome when they reached the shore. Pompey sank heavily into his seat and began practicing a speech in Greek that he had composed for the young pharaoh. As the boat scraped on the sand he rose to get out, and one of the officers stabbed him in the back. In full view of both Pompey's wife and Ptolemy XIII who was watching from the walls, the rest of the company drew their knives and started stabbing. Pompey barely made a sound. Pulling his toga up to hide his face, he swayed under the blows and then collapsed into the surf.

The head was cut off and sent to Alexandria as a present to Caesar, and the corpse was left to float into the harbour. It remained there until one of his freed slaves came and hauled it out. A funeral pyre made of the wood from a wrecked fishing boat consumed the last remains of Pompey the Great. He had been one day short of his fifty-ninth birthday.

Three days later Caesar reached Egypt.

---

[139] This obscure city was oddly important to history. It was the site – among many others – of the failure of Sennacherib's Egyptian campaign mentioned in Isaiah, of the decisive battle that ended native pharaonic control of Egypt, and the point where the bacteria responsible for the Black Death (Yersinia Pestis) first entered the Roman world during the 6th century reign of Justinian.

Chapter 21

THE LAST OF THE PTOLEMIES

"For her beauty was in itself not altogether incomparable... but converse with her had an irresistible charm"

- Plutarch

Rome may have been the political master of the Mediterranean, but Alexandria was its cultural heart. Built by Alexander the Great, it boasted numbered streets, a lighthouse that was one of the Seven Wonders of the World, and a diverse, cultured population that equalled, or surpassed, that of Rome[140]. Its great Library, whose goal was to house every book ever written, contained more than seven hundred thousand scrolls, and its scientific output alone reduced most other places to mere footnotes. Drawn by the unparalleled collection of the Library, the city drew a who's who of celebrated thinkers: the polymath Archimedes, the mathematician Eratosthenes, and Euclid, the father of geometry, among countless others[141]. Over the centuries, the city had grown into a kind of Ptolemaic playground. The curious could gawk at automatic doors powered by steam, the glass-enclosed tomb of Alexander the Great with his perfectly preserved corpse inside, and a Hall dedicated to all the works of the Muses – the world's first museum.

It was hard not to find all of this slightly intimidating. The Roman dismissiveness of the Greek east as soft and debauched was in part a defense against the cultural brilliance on display. Visiting

---

[140] Alexandria was by far the most famous of the seventy cities that Alexander named after himself. Its thriving Jewish quarter produced the Septuagint – a Greek translation of the Torah that became the most widely used version of the Scriptures by both Jewish and early Christian writers.

[141] Eratosthenes calculated the circumference of the Earth to within nine hundred miles.

Roman ambassadors took pains to rub Ptolemaic noses in the fact that they were politically impotent[142]. Caesar was no exception. He arrived with only four thousand men and promptly took over the royal palace, without even bothering to ask the king.

Ptolemy XIII was in no position to be offended. He had only recently become pharaoh, and was technically a joint ruler with his older sister Cleopatra VII. Relations between them, however, had broken down, and they were currently engaged in a civil war[143]. If he could get Caesar to endorse him as senior ruler, it would effectively settle affairs once and for all.

His opening salvo – sure to ingratiate himself with the Roman overlord – was to present Caesar with the picked head of Pompey. But instead of showing gratitude, Caesar allegedly wept. His mood grew even darker when he heard the details. Such an end to a great man was humiliating for any Roman. Caesar ordered Pompey's corpse to be located so it could be given a proper burial, and commanded both siblings to disband their armies and appear before him in the royal palace. Only then would he judge their case.

Ptolemy was not about to let his sister anywhere near Caesar. He hurried to Alexandria but instructed his army to keep Cleopatra far away. Cleopatra, however, was far more resourceful than her brother realized. She had herself smuggled through enemy lines – supposedly in a laundry bag – and into the royal palace. There, she made one of history's great entrances: the bag was opened and she sprang out with a flourish[144].

Caesar was instantly captivated. The age difference between them – she was not yet twenty-one and he was in his early fifties – was hardly important. She was witty, ruthless, and nearly as ambitious as Caesar himself. She was perhaps more attractive than beautiful by

---

[142] Cato had once spent an entire audience sitting on a toilet, forcing the embarrassed king to carry on discussions while he relieved himself.

[143] To muddy the waters further, a third sibling had used the chaos to declare herself pharaoh.

[144] The legend that she was rolled up in a carpet comes from an eighteenth century mistranslation of Plutarch.

ancient standards, but her personality was intoxicating[145]. They began their affair immediately.

Ptolemy XIII was in his early teens, and when he was informed of what his sister was up to he threw a temper tantrum worthy of the spoiled child that he was. Throwing his golden crown violently to the ground, he screamed about his trampled rights and called down curses on Caesar.

These words fell on fertile ground. The Alexandrians had long ago grown tired of strutting Romans looking down their noses at everyone else. A vague idea of "standing up" to the foreigners had been circulating for years as Rome had slowly absorbed all of their neighbors. Caesar had added fuel to the fire by commandeering the palace and cavorting – sometimes to the early hours of the morning – with Cleopatra. Even worse, he had started to siphon off funds from the treasury, allegedly to collect on a large sum that the previous pharaoh had promised to Rome.

The tipping point was Ptolemy's tirade. Caesar's troops were openly jeered in the streets, and a few were captured by a mob and lynched. For once Caesar was completely unprepared. He barricaded himself inside the palace – a vast undertaking since the complex covered nearly a third of the city – and tried to fend off the mob. His retreating men burned the Egyptian fleet in the harbour, and set fire to a few surrounding buildings to deter pursuit. Unfortunately, the flames soon spread to the Library, damaging the city's greatest treasure[146].

Caesar was now in real trouble. Even if he could have gotten past the angry crowd outside the palace, adverse winds made any escape by sea impossible. The situation got even worse when Ptolemy's army – five times the size of Caesar's meager force – joined the mob. For five

---

[145] By any standards, Cleopatra was an extraordinary person. She was credited with books on a wide range of subjects from hairdressing to philosophical inquiries, she was the first Ptolemaic ruler to learn the native Egyptian language, and she was fluent in half a dozen more. She rarely ever needed an interpreter.

[146] How extensive the damage was has been the source of much conjecture. It was completely destroyed by the seventh century.

months Caesar remained trapped in Alexandria, not able to smuggle so much as a letter out.

It appeared as if the victor of Pharsalus would face as humiliating an end as its loser. Repeated attempts to break Ptolemy's hold on the capital failed. On one occasion, Caesar only avoided capture by leaping overboard, leaving his celebrated cloak behind. The story of him swimming with one hand to preserve some papers while arrows rained down around him might have added to his legend, but it also showed how desperate he had become.

Finally, in March of 47 his long-awaited reinforcements arrived and after a short battle, Ptolemy XIII fled[147]. While attempting to sail across the Nile, his boat was overwhelmed by refugees – drawn no doubt by his conspicuous golden armour – and the ship capsized, drowning everyone on board. Cleopatra was now the only legitimate ruler, and to secure her position she married her last remaining brother, the ten-year old Ptolemy XIV.

The Egyptian civil war may have been over, but unfortunately, the larger Roman one was not. While Caesar had been stuck in Alexandria, bad news had begun to pile up. In Italy, Mark Antony's partying had managed to provoke extensive resentment against Caesar's rule, and two of Pompey's sons had managed to build up a base in Spain. More worrisome, Cato was raising a huge army in North Africa, and Mithridates' son, Pharnaces, had taken advantage of the chaos to invade Roman territory. The victory Caesar had won so dearly at Pharsalus was all but squandered.

Incredibly, Caesar refused to budge. It says a lot about his confidence – or Cleopatra's charms – that the man famous for his quick, decisive action, spent the next two months like a tourist on holiday. Cleopatra, by now heavily pregnant, escorted Caesar down the Nile in the royal pleasure yacht. The two of them nearly sailed to Ethiopia, before Caesar turned around. Although widely criticized by scandalized courtiers, there was method to Caesar's madness. He had been accompanied on his cruise by four hundred ships crammed with

---

[147] The relief force included three thousand Jews commanded by Pompey's one-time client, Antipater.

Roman soldiers. The thinly-veiled message would have been obvious to the peasants watching from the shore. Egypt and its resources belonged to him. Leaving three legions to secure Cleopatra on her throne, he set off to restore the right order to the world.

His first target was Pharnaces, who was making good use of the fact that Pompey had stripped Asia of most of its soldiers. The Pontic king had swept into what is now Turkey, determined to pull Roman settlement out by the roots. The small garrisons were crushed, and captured Roman males – nearly all of them civilians – were castrated.

Caesar now made up for his earlier delays. He marched up through Israel, stopping in Jerusalem long enough to give the Jewish strongman Antipater Roman citizenship and grant the Jews permission to rebuild the walls of the city[148]. Along the way he stripped the East of wealth to pay for his vast expenses. His justification for this would have made Machiavelli proud: "Armies need money and money is acquired by armies. If you lose one, you lose the other".

After entering Pontus, it took five days for him to find Pharnaces, and four hours to crush him completely. So much for the great eastern threat. After the battle, Caesar dryly remarked that Pompey was lucky to have won his reputation against such easy enemies. Now only Cato was left to keep the sputtering Republican hopes alive.

North Africa promised to be a much tougher nut to crack. Drawn by Cato's reputation, recruits had flooded in, and Cato, recognizing that his skills weren't in the military arena, had deferred command to Pompey's father-in-law, Metellus Scipio.

This turned out to be a shrewd move. Metellus' talent was in raising money. As Caesar somewhat admiringly put it, if a name could be found for something, he would tax it. While Caesar was cavorting with Cleopatra, Cato and Metellus had raised, equipped, and trained a staggering fourteen legions.

What unnerved Caesar's troops, however, wasn't the size of the army or the sixty war elephants drawn up beside them. What disturbed them was Metellus' name. He was a direct descendant of the man who defeated Hannibal, and a local oracle prophesied that a

---

[148] He almost certainly met Antipater's extraordinary son Herod.

Scipio would always be triumphant in Africa. Fortunately, the oracle failed to specify which Scipio would win, and Caesar, ever pragmatic, found a distant member of the family within his own ranks. Dragging the man in front of his cheering troops, he declared that as always, the gods were smiling on Caesar[149].

And so it proved. Despite being outnumbered and so short of supplies that he was forced to feed his horses washed seaweed, Caesar crushed the Republican army. It was one of his most lopsided victories; Metellus lost fifty thousand, Caesar allegedly barely fifty[150]. The only thing that marred the triumph was the unusual savagery that the winners displayed. Some ten thousand prisoners were slaughtered after the battle ended, either on Caesar's orders or because a fainting spell – a reoccurrence of his "distemper of the head" – left him unable to control his troops[151].

News of the disaster was brought to Cato in nearby Utica. He greeted the message with his customary stoic demeanour, showing neither surprise nor concern. He dined that night as usual, discussing philosophy with his companions. The topic was freedom, a particularly bitter theme since Caesar's victory had ensured its extinction. When the group at last broke up, Cato called for a copy of the Phaedo – Plato's account of Socrates' death – and retired to his room. When he was finished reading he drew a knife from where it was hidden in his robes and stabbed himself in the stomach. Unfortunately, a wound in the hand prevented him from striking a clean blow, and he thrashed around in agony, alerting his friends. His son rushed into his room to find his father lying unconscious in a pool of blood with his intestines spilling out. A doctor was immediately called, and managed to sew

---

[149] Caesar had a habit of turning bad omens to his purpose. When he had arrived on the African coast he had tripped and fallen on his face in front of his soldiers. He had declared loudly – with just a trace of humor – that Africa had risen up to embrace its conqueror.

[150] One of Caesar's casualties was an officer who was captured by the enemy. When they offered to spare him, he replied that that Caesar's men were used to giving mercy, not receiving it. Before his stunned onlookers could stop him, the man grabbed a dagger and stabbed himself to death.

[151] Some of the Pompeians fighting had already been pardoned by Caesar once, and were seen as unredeemable traitors by the men. Some of Caesar's own officers were cut down when they tried to prevent the killing.

up the wound. As soon as he woke up, however, Cato tore out the stitches – and his entrails – with his bare hands. He refused to live in a world where Caesar was all-powerful.

His death plunged Utica into mourning. At the outbreak of the war the city had been solidly in Caesar's camp, but had been won over by Cato's refusal to let his soldiers kill any locals for their support of Caesar. This desire to save what Roman lives he could was obviously sincere. When it became apparent that the cause was lost, he ordered the citizens of Utica to surrender rather than continue a doomed resistance. For Utica – and much of the Roman world – Cato would always remain a hero[152].

Caesar wept when he was informed that his most stubborn enemy was dead. He had been cheated of a grand gesture of forgiveness, which would have shown him to be the greater man. This wasn't just an act on Caesar's part. If he didn't figure out some way to discredit him, Cato's ghost would be even more formidable than the living man. As usual, Caesar moved quickly. There were a few loose ends to tie up in North Africa – and another affair to conduct with a Moorish queen named Eunoë – but he was soon on his way back to Rome.

His first action was to relieve Mark Antony of command. His lieutenant's behavior had been shockingly bad. Rome had slipped into anarchy while Antony had alternated between thuggish violence and almost comical debauchery. He had managed to alienate nearly everyone and seriously undermined Caesar's popularity. As a punishment he was stripped of all rank and kept in disgrace as a private citizen for two years.

It was now time for Caesar to concentrate on the propaganda war. In order to put all his enemies – living and dead – beneath his shadow, he threw the most lavish party the city had ever seen. Rome desperately needed a celebration. A census taken by Caesar when he returned showed that the population had declined by half during the ruinous civil war. As the writer Petronius put it, "the world itself was maimed".

---

[152] Cicero's eulogy was elegantly simple. Cato was "one of the few men who had been greater than his reputation."

Caesar rose to the occasion. Four triumphs were held in a row, each lasting for more than a week. Throughout the festivities the entire population was fed at more than twenty-two-thousand tables groaning with food set out under exotic silk awnings.

There were theatrical performances, athletic contests, and gladiator fights in the Forum, all on a scale never seen before. More than four hundred lions fought in specially designed pens, and audiences gasped at the novel sight of a camelopard, an animal never before seen in Rome[153]. There were mock battles with infantry, cavalry, and war elephants, naval campaigns on an artificial lake, and the public execution of Vercingetorix[154].

Most impressive of all were the triumphs themselves. Endless baggage trains of loot wound their way through Rome, each with placards or paintings detailing which corner of the world Caesar had conquered. Some were staggering by their size – body counts totalling more than a million – others by their magnificence. Caesar's famous wit was also present. Usually huge placards carrying descriptions of battles were paraded along with baggage trains of loot. Caesar, however, had summed up his brief campaign against Pharnaces with three words on a large sign: Veni, Vidi, Vici – I came, I saw, I conquered[155].

There was even magnanimity with victory. Included in the images displayed was one showing the death of the two officers who had murdered Pompey. The crowd roared its approval. Caesar's dedication to justice included avenging wrongs done to his enemies.

---

[153] Otherwise known as a giraffe. Nearly everything was calculated to outdo Pompey who had introduced a rhinoceros and an ape to Rome. Pompey had carried silver statues in his processions, so Caesar used gold, and so forth.

[154] A Numidian king who had allied with Cato was also slated to be executed, but he had committed suicide before he could be captured. His four year old son was displayed in the parade instead, and – to the delight of the crowd – thoroughly enjoyed himself. One Roman writer called him the "happiest captive" he had ever seen. The crowd was thrilled when the child was released in a show of Caesar's magnanimity.

[155] It also included a painting of Pharnaces running away which was greeted by much laughter.

There was, however, one discordant note. One of the floats that was carried through the streets depicted Cato committing suicide. It was intended to be monstrous; a villain ripping out his own intestines. Instead, it moved the population to pity. Many openly wept. The rest simply watched it pass by in silence.

It was a misstep by Caesar, but only a minor one. For most Romans the performance was a resounding success, particularly since as a finale he handed out vast sums of money. Each soldier was awarded the equivalent of forty years' salary, and every citizen got gifts of money, wheat, and olive oil. The festivities concluded with a vast banquet, at the end of which Caesar was escorted home by forty elephants bearing torches in their trunks.

The Senate rushed to heap honors on him. For the third time he was made a dictator, this time for an unprecedented period of ten years. Since he was also the sole consul, he had more constitutional power than anyone else in Roman history. He justified this with an ambitious program that demonstrated what effective leadership could do. He reduced the number of slaves in Italy, drastically cut state expenses, and extended citizenship to all doctors and teachers living in Rome[156]. Eighty thousand of the jobless poor who had been such a source of political volatility were granted land in overseas colonies, and the Senate was increased to nearly a thousand members[157]. Work was started on a codification of Roman law, eventually completed in the sixth century by Justinian, and two libraries – one for Greek works and the other for Latin – were commissioned[158]. Marshes were drained, highways were built, and canals were cut. Most enduringly of all, the calendar was fixed.

Like nearly all Mediterranean cultures, Rome based its calendar on a lunar model of roughly three hundred and fifty-five days. This meant that over time the calendar would become hopelessly out of

---

[156] He also extended citizenship to Transalpine Gaul which officially unified the Italian peninsula. It wouldn't be united again until 1871.
[157] The old patrician families became a minority in the Senate. The new enrollees included former slaves, veterans, and even some foreigners.
[158] His old Spanish enemy Varro was given the task of classifying and systematizing these works.

sync with the actual seasons, so an intercalary month of twenty days or so had to be periodically added between February and March. Thanks to the Civil War, no correction had been made for at least six years, so that the coldest months were now in the "summer". As Pontifex Maximus, Caesar was responsible for this, so he decided to institute a permanent solution. He designed a more precise calendar based on the Egyptian solar model, brought it in line with the seasons, and added a leap day every four years[159]. In gratitude, the seventh month, Quintilis, was renamed July in his honor.

And yet, despite all his power, it was not all smooth sailing. Brutus caused a minor scandal when he divorced his wife to marry the dead Cato's daughter, Porcia[160]. Caesar lost his temper and wrote a blistering attack called the Anti-Cato where he portrayed his dead foe as an insane drunk. This uncharacteristically tin-eared effort was widely mocked for the smear it obviously was, and Cato's reputation only increased.

It was almost a relief when news arrived that winter from Spain. Pompey's two sons had rallied their father's veterans and driven out Caesar's generals. Virtually the entire province was now in the hands of the rebels. He left immediately.

---

[159] Caesar had clearly been thinking about this for some time. He brought up the topic at a banquet in Alexandria, and was greatly assisted by Egyptian scientists. His calendar – with one small change by Pope Gregory XIII in 1582 – is still in use today by most of the world.

[160] He failed to give any legitimate reason for the divorce other than a desire to marry his cousin, Porcia.

Chapter 22

DICTATOR

"We are his slaves, but he is the slave of the times"

- Cicero

Caesar moved with his customary speed, covering more than fifteen hundred miles in less than a month. This campaign, however, was unlike any other he had fought. He arrived in December and found the situation serious enough to warrant a winter offensive. This meant that he had to fight in appalling conditions – heavy snows and freezing rains – while simultaneously finding enough food for the army.

This would have been difficult under any circumstances, but Caesar was also nearing exhaustion. The customary magnanimity was gone, replaced by brutal savagery[161]. The heads of defeated soldiers were paraded on poles and their corpses were used as building materials. There was no safe haven in surrender for Pompey's sons, and no citizenship for his defeated soldiers. To stand against Caesar was to be utterly crushed.

The Pompeian army at first refused to offer a pitched battle, preferring guerrilla tactics to bleed their enemy dry. Two months of relentless pressure, however, convinced Pompey's sons to risk a pitched battle on the plains of Munda in southern Spain.

The two sides were equally matched, but the Pompeians fought with a frenzied desperation. During the eight hours of intense fighting, things got so bleak for Caesar that he briefly considered suicide. As

---

[161] Many of the veteran troops facing him had already been pardoned once, and he was not in the mood to make a second offer.

he said later, he had fought many times for victory, but at Munda he fought for his life.

The turning point came when Caesar, who was commanding the right wing of his army, began to push the Pompeians back. Pompey's son tried to shore up his line by shifting troops from the opposite wing, but this critically weakened it. Caesar, who had noticed the maneuvering, sent his cavalry crashing into the thinned wing and the line broke. The Pompeians fled in confusion, and what had been an evenly matched contest turned into a bloody rout. A few managed to find safety within the walls of Munda, the rest – some thirty thousand men – lay dead on the battlefield.

The Spanish victory marked the effective end of the civil war. Pompey's younger son, Sextus, escaped and tried to regroup in Sicily, but there was little he could do. The conservative cause was dead, and wouldn't be revived. But Spain had also shaken Caesar. He had come face to face with his own mortality, and there were few who better understood how fine a line there was between victory and death. There were other reasons to be reflective. His health was showing signs of deteriorating. Earlier that year he had had another fainting spell, becoming momentarily powerless while listening to a speech by Cicero. He was about to turn fifty-five, the same age that his father had died, and his only legitimate child was dead.

Sometime after the battle, Caesar was joined by his eighteen-year old grand-nephew, Gaius Octavius. The boy had begged his mother to be allowed to join his grand-uncle, and despite a serious illness and a shipwreck along the way, had hurried to the front. He was hardly an impressive figure to look at. Thanks to chronic sickness he was pale and thin, of average height with brown eyes and widely-spaced teeth. He was neither athletic nor particularly coordinated, and certainly wasn't at home in a military camp.

Physically, he couldn't have been more different than his grand-uncle, yet behind his eyes was an almost frightening intelligence. There is no record of their conversation, but Caesar recognized a familiar iron will in this extraordinary teen. He was pleased enough to invite Octavius to share his carriage on the trip back to Rome.

They arrived to find a minor scandal brewing. In Caesar's absence, Cleopatra had breezed into the city with an immense train of servants. She was accompanied by her husband-brother and her one-year old son who she had provocatively named Ptolemy Caesar[162]. Although it was an open secret who the boy's father was – he was popularly known as Caesarion – Caesar officially denied it, and one of his friends felt obliged to publish a pamphlet arguing that he couldn't possibly have fathered the child[163]. Cleopatra, however, wasn't about to be pushed aside. She installed herself in Caesar's mansion, paying no attention at all to Caesar's wife, Calpurnia.

If Caesar was embarrassed, he certainly didn't show it. After depositing a new will with the Vestal Virgins, he took Cleopatra on vacation for two months. A rumor that he planned to marry her and move the capital to Egypt began to circulate. It got even louder when Caesar erected a golden statue of his mistress in the Temple of Venus. There was a growing sense that he had been seduced by the East. What was next, deification?

A disturbingly un-Roman note began to seep into his behavior. He celebrated a fifth triumph for the Spanish campaign, despite the fact that triumphs were reserved for victories over foreign nations not Roman legions commanded by a rival general. Massive silver floats depicting the defeat of the Pompeians only underscored how out of touch all of this was. The historian Plutarch wrote a century or so later that these actions turned the Romans against him because they glorified the destruction of the family of one of the greatest men of Rome.

There were other warning signs. In one of the staged productions to celebrate the event, an actor pointedly looked at Caesar when he said the line, "He whom many fear must fear many". The dictator may have filed it away, but he said nothing.

The Senate, spineless as ever, continued to pile on honors. He only accepted a fraction of what they offered, but it was still

---

[162] An often overlooked fact is that by naming her son Caesar, she was openly admitting that he was a bastard. It was a perfect example of her *realpolitik*. The alliance with Rome was more important than dynastic legitimacy.

[163] Caesarion means "little Caesar".

embarrassing. An ivory statue of him straddling the globe was set up in the Temple of Romulus and another was put somewhat ominously among the statues of the kings. He was voted the titles of "Liberator", "Prefect of Morals", and "Father of the Country", by senators who seemed in a kind of frenzied contest to ingratiate themselves[164].

The more time that passed, the more ludicrous the awards became. His image was placed on coins – the first living Roman so honoured – and he was given the right to be permanently hailed as Imperator[165]. The crescendo was reached late in the year 45. The Senate declared that his birthday was a national holiday, and made him semi-divine, dedicating a temple to his clemency and a college of priests to honour him[166].

Caesar's reaction to all this was disdain. If there had ever been a doubt that the Republic was dead, it was now dispelled. The thought that these sniveling pygmies could ever be trusted with the task of governing – or have the courage to act on principle – was laughable. Even in public, the mask began to slip. When a group of senators approached him and offered him more lavish awards, he dryly responded that his "honors needed diminishing more than increasing"[167]. He took to quoting a line from Euripides that "tyranny is the noblest crime". Absolute power, in other words, was a cause worth pursuing, even if it disturbed those of lesser imagination. He was shockingly open about his view of the Republic. Even Sulla at the

[164] Appointing Caesar – a well-known womanizer who had seduced a large portion of Rome's elite women – Prefect of Morals, was particularly rich. It was made more so by his well-known??According to Tacitus, there were still Gallic noblemen claiming to be descended from him more than a century after his death.

[165] Although the English word "emperor" comes from this word, during Republican times it merely meant 'one who commands'. Victorious Roman generals were forbidden from using the title after they had celebrated their triumph.

[166] The line between mortal and divine was much blurrier for the Romans than it is for monotheistic religions. There were various levels of divinity that were recognized in the West. In the East, Caesar was already worshipped as a full god. One surviving inscription in the city of Ephesus says *Julius Caesar… a god who has appeared among us for the salvation of all mankind."*

[167] He famously refused to rise for the senators – a serious breach of courtesy. The reason for this has been hotly debated ever since; Caesar himself claimed that he felt one of his periodic fits of weakness and didn't want to disgrace himself by collapsing in front of them.

height of his dictatorship scrupulously pretended that he was serving the Republic's interests. But not Caesar. "What is the Republic?" he asked bitingly. "a nothingness, a name only, without body or substance".

The Republic had drowned in a sea of corruption, violence, and incompetence. The men who claimed to govern it now were squabbling children in desperate need of an adult to lead them. It was an open secret; Caesar had just been the first to say it out loud. There were undoubtedly relics like Cicero wringing their hands, but they too had voted to deify Caesar. There seemed no need to hide the fact that he was the master of Rome.

When a tribune whom he had pardoned decided to protest tyranny by not standing when he approached, Caesar mockingly dared him to "come take back the Republic from me". In private, he called Sulla "an ignorant child" for resigning his dictatorship, and menacingly snapped at an insubordinate senator that men should "treat my word as law".

He began to appear in public wearing the high red boots once worn by Rome's ancient kings, as well as a purple cloak and a golden wreath on his head[168]. All he needed now was the title of king.

Even his famous magnanimity carried a whiff of royalty. Technically, only the Senate could pardon a criminal; Caesar's disregard of this was a reminder of his power. For many proud Republicans, a pardon was more galling than death. Cato wasn't the only one who would echo the Spartan sentiment that it was better to die on your feet than to live on your knees. The forgiveness of Caesar was a hard thing to forgive.

In the shadows, a coalition began to form. It was led – appropriately enough – by a triumvirate of men. The main instigator was Cassius Longinus, a man who had been nursing a grudge against Caesar for a decade. He had been an active opponent as a tribune, and had been one of the first to enlist with Pompey during the Civil

---

[168] Ironically, as 'Prefect of Morals' he had passed a luxury law banning purple robes along with any other ostentatious display.

War[169]. Caesar's clemency only seemed to harden Cassius' hatred. Despite an official pardon after Pharsalus and an appointment to several important posts including a stint as governor of Syria, Cassius remained convinced that Caesar was a dangerous tyrant.

Caesar himself seemed completely oblivious. In February of 44 BC the Senate proclaimed him dictator for life, and he decided to test the waters of kingship. On the 15th of that month, he appeared in public dressed like Jupiter and sat on a golden throne in the rostrum to watch the Lupercalia, an ancient festival of purification which probably predated the Republic itself[170]. In a carefully staged performance Mark Antony offered Caesar a crown which he ostentatiously refused. A few voices urged him to accept, but cheering broke out when he declined. Antony repeated the offer and the crowd groaned. With a flash of annoyance – for the crowd's reaction or the offer – he pushed it away again, and more cheers broke out.

A week later, Cassius invited his brother-in-law, Marcus Junius Brutus to dinner[171]. His guest had become one of the most well-respected Romans of the day. He was a philosopher and a proud aristocrat, determined to live up to the strict moral example of his father-in-law Cato. History weighed heavily on Brutus. He was a descendant of Lucius Junius Brutus, the celebrated founder of the Roman Republic who had overthrown the tyrannical last king of Rome, and sacrificed his own family for the well-being of the state.

Cassius didn't have to do much convincing. Despite his stoic preventions, Brutus was a man of impatiently strong emotions. As Caesar had once put it, "whatever Brutus wants, he wants badly".

The trouble was that Brutus was torn between admiring Caesar and despising him. The tipping point had come a few days before when a crown had been discovered on one of Caesar's statues. A citizen had loudly saluted it as king, but had been immediately arrested by two

---

[169] He accompanied Crassus on the Parthian campaign and may have partially blamed Caesar for the disaster. His wife had an affair with Caesar, although this seems to have played little part in their feud.

[170] An alternate name of the festival was *dies Februatus* which gave the month its name.

[171] Ironically, it was Caesar's preferential treatment of Brutus that was the main cause of Cassius' disaffection with Caesar.

tribunes who had also removed the crown. The tribunes themselves were then arrested by Caesar on the weak grounds that they had denied him the opportunity to remove the crown himself.

The tribunes immediately became popular heroes, and the mob began to refer to them as "Brutuses" for their stance against tyranny. That night firebrands had scrawled graffiti over the speaker's platform and chair where Brutus sat with slogans like "Wake up!" and "You are no Brutus!". This finally stung him into action. On the night of February 22, he joined the plot to kill Caesar.

The third member of the murderous triumvirate was a distant cousin of Marcus named Decimus Brutus. Unlike his relative, Decimus had always been a partisan of Caesar. His betrayal was in many ways the most bitter. Decimus' parents had nearly ruined the family, and Caesar had offered him a chance to rebuild his fortunes. Decimus had served loyally in Gaul and had been with Caesar through some of his most difficult campaigns. He had held the line in Alesia and walked with Caesar in his triumph. Ambition, however, had turned him against the dictator. There was no chance of his own triumph or even an ovation with the great man clogging the way.

The conspirators now faced the problem of how to get rid of Caesar. Secrecy was obviously most important, but since their aim was to remove a tyrant, not stage a coup, it had to appear legitimate. This meant involving as many important officials as possible while simultaneously preventing leaks. Cicero was briefly considered, before being rejected for lacking the requisite courage, as well as being a known blabbermouth. Somewhat surprisingly, Mark Antony was also considered. He had been approached a year earlier for a different conspiracy, and although he had chosen to stay loyal, he had left his options open by not informing Caesar either.

In the end, about sixty senators joined the conspiracy, most of whom had taken Caesar's side during the Civil War. Some joined because they felt Caesar had belittled them or stunted their political careers, others because of genuine concerns for the Republic. Liberty was the watchword of revolution.

Caesar, meanwhile, had helpfully dismissed his bodyguards with the comment that "it was better to die once than to live always expecting death". He seemed in a perpetual hurry, anxious to move from one grand plan to the next. He had already built a new forum, now he announced plans for a new library, a theater that would dwarf Pompey's, and the construction of the largest temple in the world on the field of Mars.

Before any of this could be completed, however, there was one more campaign to fight. Crassus' death was still unavenged, and – more importantly – his lost standards still graced some Parthian temple. Rectifying this national humiliation was both politically savvy and Caesar's duty as dictator. A law allowing him to appoint all magistrates without the bother of time-consuming elections was passed, and a departure date was set for March 18th[172].

The conspirators realized that they had to act fast. The invasion of Parthia would take several years at a minimum, and Caesar would return at the head of an army. The Ides of March – three days before his departure – was chosen. It was a resonant date. The Ides were traditionally seen as the day to settle debts.

On the evening of the 14th of March, Caesar dined with Lepidus and Decimus Brutus. As the evening progressed, Caesar turned the conversation to the topic of mortality. He asked his companions what sort of death was ideal, and listened as they amiably debated. When the question was put to him, he answered with a single word: suddenly. That night, his long-suffering wife, Calpurnia, had a nightmare of him drenched in blood, and woke up in a panic. She begged her husband not to meet with the Senate, but to send the recently pardoned Antony in his stead. For once, Caesar was unnerved. This was out of character for his usually sedate wife. The morning's sacrifice had been ominous, and perhaps he remembered that a few days earlier an Etruscan soothsayer had warned him that his

---

[172] As part of his preparations for the campaign, Caesar decided to dig a canal through the isthmus of Corinth. An architect was appointed and drew up plans, but the project was abandoned after Caesar's death. It wasn't completed until 1893.

life would be in danger through the Ides. Bowing to her entreaties, he called for Antony to dismiss the Senate.

Before Antony could leave, however, Decimus Brutus arrived, and successfully mocked Caesar for listening to a woman's fears. If he wanted to dismiss the Senate, he argued, then Caesar ought to at least have the courtesy to do it in person. They were carried by litters to Pompey's theater complex where the Senate was meeting in one of the temples[173]. As they crossed through the Forum, Caesar is supposed to have spied the soothsayer that had warned him and called out that the Ides of March had come. The diviner shot back, "yes, Caesar, but they have not yet gone".

Pompey's magnificent theater was being used for some games as Caesar arrived, and the roar could clearly be heard. He headed for an adjacent building where the Senate was meeting, and there received one final warning: as he walked towards the entrance to the temple a crowd gathered around him and a Greek teacher from Brutus' household pressed a note into his hand with details about the plot. Caesar, thinking it was yet another petition, neglected to read it. As Appian rather poetically put it, "Caesar had to suffer Caesar's fate".

One of the conspirators drew Antony aside to prevent him from interfering, and the rest crowded around Caesar as he made his way towards his golden chair. A senator named Lucius Cimber asked for the recall of a brother that the dictator had exiled. The rest of the assassins crowded around him as if to support the petition, clasping his hands. Suddenly Cimber grabbed Caesar's toga and violently wrenched it down to expose the neck, shouting "what are you waiting for?". A knife slashed at Caesar's throat but missed and struck him in the shoulder.

Caesar fought back furiously, using the stylus he was carrying to stab his assailant. He grabbed hold of the man's arm and hurled him to the ground. But there were too many of them. As Caesar lurched forward a knife stabbed into his side and another flashed at his throat.

---

[173] Just after Caesar left his house that morning a slave supposedly arrived with news of the assassination. He was given permission to wait until Caesar returned.

In the confusion some of the conspirators stabbed each other, but most blows rained down on the dictator.

Caesar began to weaken, but still thrashed about until Brutus stabbed him in the groin. Seeing the son of his favourite mistress he asked "You too, my son?" in Greek and stopped struggling. Pulling his toga over his head to hide the death agony, he collapsed at the foot of a statue of Pompey the Great.

As blood oozed from the twenty-three stab wounds, the disheveled assassins addressed the watching senators[174]. Brutus, his hair dishevelled, and his toga blood-spattered, hailed Cicero as the "Father of the Country" and called on him to lead the restored Republic. In response, the orator, and hundreds of his horrified colleagues fled.

It was a telling reaction, if only the assassins had been wise enough to see it. It was one thing to overthrow a tyrant, and quite another to recover liberty.

---

[174] Suetonius claimed that an autopsy was done by a doctor who concluded that only one of the wounds was fatal.

Chapter 23

AFTERMATH

"Did I save these men that they might murder me?"

- Caesar

For a moment, the assassins, or liberators as they called themselves, were left standing in an empty chamber. The reaction of their colleagues was disappointing but understandable. A public assassination was not for the faint of heart. But now that the deed was done, the celebrations would surely follow. It was a heady moment. With the stroke of a knife Brutus had restored the Republic. He had answered the call of history and lived up to his famous name. All that remained was to let Rome know the tyrant was dead.

One of the liberators produced a cap worn by slaves when they gained their freedom, and Brutus mounted it on a pole. Brandishing it, they all marched up to the Capitol waving their bloody knives and shouting the good news. Caesar was dead, the Republic was saved, and all of Rome was now free!

It should have been the supreme moment of triumph for Brutus. Caesar's allies were in hiding or had fled, and most of the Senate supported his action. Yet his proclamation of freedom was met by stunned silence that was only broken by screams from the direction of Pompey's theater. The spectators had realized what had happened and pandemonium had broken out as they tried to claw their way over each other to escape the complex. In the streets, rioters began to loot stores, smashing doors and setting fire to buildings. Some unfortunates were crushed in the chaos as most citizens thought of nothing more than barricading themselves inside their own homes.

Under cover of the general confusion, three of Caesar's slaves snuck into the room where his corpse lay, and managed to carry it home. There it was washed and given the customary preparation for cremation.

Cicero, meanwhile, had recovered his nerve, and congratulated the liberators, urging them to be ruthless in finishing the job. By this he meant Antony and Lepidus. Now was the time to utterly destroy the regime. As long as any prominent supporter was alive, Caesar's veterans would have a leader to rally around, and the threat of tyranny would still exist.

Unbelievably, Brutus couldn't see this[175]. There was no plan beyond killing Caesar, no proposals for addressing the rampant corruption or curbing the army's role in politics. It was as if he thought all the evil in the world was contained in one man, and removing him would restore all that was good. A flabbergasted Cicero summed up the liberators as having "the spirits of men, but the foresight of children"[176].

Belatedly, Brutus realized that he needed to convert the people of Rome to his side. The leading assassins went to the Forum and addressed a crowd that had gathered. To make them more pliable, Brutus distributed money liberally, and then repeated his sentiments about liberty. There was something hopelessly naive about this. As the Roman historian Appian pointed out, Brutus expected two contradictory things from the people; that they should want to be free and at the same time take bribes.

There were a few lackluster cheers, but by now it was clear that the liberators had squandered whatever advantage they had. Antony, realizing that his life was not immediately in danger, came out of hiding and asked to meet with them. The next day, during a private gathering in the Senate House, a tentative truce was agreed to between the assassins and Caesar's partisans. There would be no bloodshed or proscriptions. The tyrant was dead, and as a sign of their

---

[175] Cassius had argued for killing other key figures of the regime as well, but Brutus overruled him on the grounds that they were executing a tyrant in the name of freedom not starting a bloodbath.

[176] Ironically, the assassins had excluded Cicero from their ranks partly because they believed that he wasn't ruthless enough.

high-mindedness, his assassins would allow men like Antony to go about their lives in peace.

It was a terrible mistake. Antony had none of the reticence of Brutus, and he acted swiftly. He already had the respect of Caesar's soldiers, and he had good reason to believe that he was Caesar's heir. Despite his recent fall from grace, Caesar clearly had trusted him, and he had been fully rehabilitated. It was a common practice for a man with no recognized children to adopt someone in their will, and Antony was clearly the most capable of his lieutenants. All he had to do was secure the document before a rival destroyed it.

Caesar's will itself was lodged with the Vestal Virgins, but there were several steps to be taken before Antony could retrieve it. His first stop was to visit Caesar's widow, Calpurnia, and collect the great man's papers and money. She turned them over immediately – yet another sign that he was Caesar's chosen successor. Then Antony secretly summoned Caesar's veterans to Rome.

The next two days were a whirlwind of activity. Antony convened the Senate and convinced them to ratify all of Caesar's acts and legislation. This was easy enough to do, since it had benefited most of them in some way, and was an easy way to appear magnanimous. Even Brutus approved the measure. The Senate also approved Caesar's will – as yet unread – and voted a public funeral for him, with Antony scheduled to give the eulogy. To cap off the newfound spirit of reconciliation, Antony dined that night with Cassius[177].

On March 19th, four days after the murder, Mark Antony retrieved Caesar's will from the Vestal Virgins and took it to the Senate. There he had a herald read the long list of honours that the Senate had voted Caesar along with the oath that everyone had sworn – including the assassins – to preserve his life. As the senators squirmed, Antony then read the will.

It exploded like a landmine. Decimus Brutus, along with several other of the assassins were beneficiaries, and even named as guardians to any future sons he may have had. Caesar's extensive pleasure

---

[177] This was somewhat awkward since several days before Cassius had argued for Antony's murder.

gardens along the Tiber were to be given to the people along with a lump sum of cash to every citizen. The remainder of his vast fortune was to be distributed among his three grandnephews, with the bulk going to his favourite, Octavius. To Antony's surprise and fury, he was not the heir. That was reserved for Octavius as well.

After the initial shock, Antony recovered his equilibrium. Octavius was a mere boy of eighteen and nowhere near Rome[178]. He could be neutralized easily enough. Caesar's veterans were in the city, and the final act of the pageant was ready to be performed.

The next day, Caesar's body was carried through the streets to be cremated and interred next to his daughter Julia on the Field of Mars. As planned, Antony gave the eulogy. He spoke briefly but brilliantly, reminding the crowd of the greatness of the slain man, and his tireless efforts to serve Rome[179]. As a grand finale, Antony dramatically seized the blood-stained toga from the corpse and displayed it – along with a wax effigy showing all twenty-three stab wounds – to the crowd. His words had the desired effect. The mood began to visibly darken. By now the contents of the will were widely known, and hundreds of veterans were interspersed with the mob. The corpse was escorted to the Forum and a bier was constructed out of whatever was handy. In an unmistakable message, the chairs reserved for the magistrates were smashed, as were senatorial benches to provide fuel for the fire.

As the flames rose, a kind of frenzy took over. Veterans tore off their cloaks and armor and threw them into the fire; women tossed their finest jewelry; actors threw their costumes, and musicians their instruments. Mobs headed for the houses of the conspirators, and several people were lynched. The liberators slipped out of the city under the cover of night.

Mark Antony had managed events brilliantly, and seemed poised to take up Caesar's power. The only thing in his way was the boy Gaius Octavius, but unfortunately for Antony, he turned out to be much more formidable than anyone had envisaged. Entering Rome

---

[178] He was in what is now Albania, finishing up his military education and preparing for the invasion of Parthia where he was due to serve as Caesar's second in command.

[179] Shakespeare's version preserves the spirit if not the exact words of Antony.

against the advice of virtually everyone, he jumped into the lethal political knife fight.

His entry immediately changed the game. Caesar's veterans were faced with a dilemma over who they should back. The abrasive Antony was a known quantity, an effective leader who had fought by their sides, earned their trust, and proven he could win. Octavius, on the other hand, though just a boy, was Caesar's heir and – equally importantly – his namesake. He had legally changed his name to Gaius Julius Caesar. How could loyal veterans fail to join him much less fight against him?

Relations between the two of them quickly broke down, and as the weeks passed, Caesar's veterans increasingly began to desert Antony for Octavius. The Senate, led by Cicero, realized that this was a perfect opportunity to destroy Caesar's legacy. If they could manipulate open warfare between the two Caesarean factions, they could use the inexperienced Octavius to crush Antony, and then rule through the weak-willed teenager.

When Antony left Rome to attack some assassins in Gaul, he was declared a public outlaw by a vote of the Senate, and Octavius was sent out to destroy him. The teenager, however, was astute enough to realize that the main beneficiary of this campaign would be the Senate, and so instead of trying to crush Antony, he arranged a meeting with him.

The two came to a private agreement that they would form an alliance, punish those who had killed Caesar, and then carve up the Roman world between them. With the forces of Caesar once again united, neither the disorganized assassins, nor the feckless Senate stood a chance.

Men like Cicero began to wonder what killing Caesar had even been for. "Freedom has been restored" he wrote in bewilderment, "and yet the Republic has not". Rome had traded the statesmanship of Caesar for the excesses of Antony and the cold calculations of Octavius. There was a growing sense that an age had ended. Caesar had been a gigantic figure, and even his enemies seemed larger than life. Antony, Octavius, and Brutus, by contrast, seemed like pygmies fighting among the ruins.

Even that fighting, however, didn't last long. Against the veteran legions of Caesar, the ill-prepared and scattered assassins – still calling themselves liberators – were quickly thrown back. By the end of the summer they had fled Italy, and within three years virtually all of them were dead. Most who weren't killed in battle committed suicide with the same knives they had used to kill Caesar.

Victory against the conspirators, however, failed to bring peace. The Mediterranean-spanning Republic apparently wasn't big enough for both Antony and Octavius. In 33 BC the truce between them officially expired, and it wasn't renewed. Rome braced itself for another civil war. All the worst practices of the past hundred years – the proscriptions and murder – were renewed with increased savagery. Roman armies hurled themselves against each other with none of the restraint or clemency that had marked Caesar's campaigns. With Antony and Octavius, a century of civil wars came to a blood-soaked crescendo.

In the end, Octavius triumphed. His rival committed suicide rather than face capture, and left the Roman world to be administered by one man. Octavius was awarded the title of Augustus – the revered one – and with peace at last secured he resigned many of his more flashy powers, and declared the Republic restored.

But something profound had changed. Augustus cared nothing for the appearance of power and everything for its substance. The Republic that he oversaw was democratic only in name. All important decisions were made by one man, and one man only. Ever conscious of the fate of Caesar, Augustus wore his mask well. During his lifetime he was known simply as princeps – the first citizen – but history remembers him as the first emperor. A new age had begun. The Roman Republic was dead; the Roman Empire had been born.

EPILOGUE

"Ambition should be made of sterner stuff"

- Shakespeare

What, in the end, are we to make of Caesar? There is a certain ambiguity to his assassination because those who feared Caesar as a tyrant and those who praised him as a savior both had a point. Caesar was a monarch in everything but name, and ruled, as he himself put it, as if his word was law. To a traditional Roman like Brutus who equated the word 'king' with slavery, this was indeed the destruction of liberty and the death of the Republic.

But Caesar was also a beacon of hope. Rome had been at war with itself for nearly a hundred years, drowning in successive bloodbaths of political violence and military coups. Caesar had correctly recognized that the solution to this murderous instability was a strong leader, and he offered an enlightened, merciful rule. If he ran roughshod over the Roman constitution in the process, that was only because it was necessary.

Caesar is a polarizing figure in another way. His life is the great dividing line in Roman history; before him was the Republic, and after him the empire. His life, therefore, asks the disquieting question of how democratic governments die. The answer, too often given, is that in Rome's case Caesar himself was the culprit. But the truth is that the Republic withered from within.

Long before Caesar was born, Roman writers were warning that society was becoming unglued. A corrupt political ruling class governing in its own interest ensured the misery of the ruled which in turn was exploited by demagogues. Political violence, unthinkable in the second century became routine in the first. A kind of moral rot had set in, and the vice at the top had a corrosive effect on those below. Men forgot their political responsibilities and sold their loyalty for the pleasures of bread and circuses.

Freedom was difficult and messy. It required sacrifice and above all service to the greater good of Rome. For most of Rome's ruling class, however, – Brutus and the assassins included – patriotism had long since dissolved into pragmatism. Caesar may have crossed the Rubicon, but far more troubling for the Republic was how willingly his soldiers followed. It was worth asking the question, were such a people even capable of being free?

Cicero put this to the Romans in the months after Caesar's death. "Life is not merely a matter of breathing", he thundered, "Other nations can endure servitude but Rome cannot"[180]. But the appeals to the old Roman virtues of liberty and service to the common good fell on deaf ears. Moral courage, like muscles, atrophy when not exercised. The ideals of the Republic were too costly for most citizens to pay. It was far easier to let Mark Antony or Augustus shoulder the burden of governing. As the poet Sallust put it, "only a few prefer liberty – the majority seek nothing more than fair masters".

Cicero eventually came to a similar conclusion. Reflecting on the last years of the Republic, he clinically diagnosed the cause of its collapse: "The fruit of too much liberty is slavery"[181]. Rome was now caught in a vicious cycle. Chaos allowed despotism to rise, and despotic rule in turn corroded the ability to be free. In rejecting Caesar's limited despotism, the Romans had merely paved the way for the far greater tyranny of Augustus.

The tragedy is that Caesar was one of history's genuinely great figures. He was perhaps the most complete man that the ancient world ever produced, equally at home on the battlefield and in the political arena. He was an architect and a legislator, a gifted orator and a writer, a man of action and a thinker. His great fault is often claimed to be an excess of ambition, but in this he was no different than countless

---

[180] This speech, directed against Mark Antony, cost Cicero his life.

[181] Cicero is summarizing Plato who argued in The Republic that "*The excess of liberty, in states or individuals, seems only to pass into slavery… and the most aggravated form of tyranny arises out of the most extreme forms of liberty*".

generations of Romans before him. Like all patricians he wanted to be the first man in Rome; the pre-eminent man in politics, wealth, and reputation. The only difference was that for Caesar the stakes were higher and – thanks to the breakdown of tradition – the restraints fewer than for previous generations[182].

Where Caesar stands apart from his contemporaries is his statesmanship. Those who came before him – and after – unleashed bloodshed when they triumphed. There were proscriptions and killings, murder and public executions. Caesar offered clemency. It may have been self-serving, but it was also a genuine attempt to break the cycle of violence that had poisoned the Republic.

Unfortunately, this experiment wasn't given more time to mature. Unlike his successor, who spent more than four decades pulling the strings, Caesar had no time to build a lasting peace. He left only the faintest sketch of what he intended behind.

In the short term his star faded. The emperor Augustus made great use of his connection to Caesar when he was gaining power, but once he was secure on the throne the opposite was true. The great conceit of his reign was that he had restored the Republic; all associations with Caesar were quietly downplayed[183]. Brutus and Cato, on the other hand, were partially rehabilitated as noble defenders of the liberty that Augustus had "restored". Yet he was unwilling to push this too far; Caesar was, after all, the founder of the dynasty.

Those who came after Augustus were not so conflicted. The Ides of March was known afterwards as 'The Day of Parricide' and the Senate never again met on that day. During the Middle Ages, Caesar was counted as one of the Nine Worthies – the nine greatest rulers of all time,[184] while Dante put Brutus and Cassius in the lowest level of hell, vile betrayers condemned to be chewed on by a monstrous Satan for eternity. Caesar's Commentaries on the Gallic Wars became

---

[182] The Roman Republic had no written constitution, instead it relied on centuries of custom and precedent to restrain ambition.

[183] Augustus turned the room in which Caesar was murdered into a communal toilet to prevent it from becoming a shrine to the assassins.

[184] There were three Jewish, three pagan, and three Christian rulers. Caesar's comrades were Hector and Alexander the Great.

the standard text for generations of Latin students, and Renaissance thinkers generally praised him as a man of letters.

Enlightenment figures were more ambivalent. As Republics struggled to be born among the absolute monarchies of Europe, Brutus and Cato became more virtuous, and Caesar more villainous. The divide was felt even by the American founding fathers. When George Washington feared that the patriot cause was lost at Valley Forge he staged a production of the play "Cato" by Joseph Addison, to inspire his troops[185]. Alexander Hamilton, meanwhile, famously called Caesar "the greatest man who ever lived".

The monarchies of Europe tended to agree with Hamilton. Both the First and Second French Empire looked directly to Caesar, and Napoleon went so far as to claim that his entire career had been inspired by the great dictator. His nephew, Napoleon III said that God "had raised up Caesar to show people the path they ought to follow"[186]. At the start of the twentieth century, three of the world's most powerful nations had rulers whose titles still bore his name[187].

The ambiguities of Caesar endlessly fascinate. Over the years he has been interpreted and reinterpreted to fit the sensibilities of the moment. He has starred as enlightened ruler and power-mad autocrat, as a debauched tyrant, and a military genius. Each generation casts him in their own mould.

Remarkably – and virtually uniquely among figures of antiquity – Caesar also speaks for himself. To open his Commentaries is to feel a charisma undimmed by twenty centuries. Few who have read it have managed to escape that magnetic pull. Shakespeare, the English language's greatest artisan, and one of Caesar's most penetrating observers, described him as "a colossus, standing bestride the narrow world".

---

[185] Ironically, the king they were revolting against – George III – had acted in the same play almost three decades earlier to protest the despotism of his father. The play is probably the source of several famous quotes by the American Founding Fathers including "Give me liberty or give me death!" and "I only regret that I have but one life to lose for my country".

[186] Napoleon III spent several years of his reign composing a two volume biography of Caesar.

[187] The German Kaiser, the Austrian Kaiser and the Russian Czar.

And so he remains. Still instantly familiar more than two thousand years after his death.

Made in the USA
Las Vegas, NV
21 January 2026